Reminders of God

Reminders of God
Altars for Personal and Family Devotion

ANNE F. GRIZZLE

PARACLETE PRESS
Brewster, Massachusetts

Scripture excerpts are taken from the HOLY BIBLE, NEW INTERNATIONAL VERSION®. Copyright © 1973, 1978, 1984 by International Bible Society. Used by permission of Zondervan Publishing House. All rights reserved. The "NIV" and "New International Version" trademarks are registered in the United States Patent and Trademark Office by International Bible Society. Use of either trademark requires the permission of International Bible Society.

Library of Congress Cataloging–in–Publication Data
Grizzle, Anne F., 1955-
    Reminders of God : altars for personal and family devotion / Anne F. Grizzle.
        p.   cm.
   ISBN 1–55725–402–8 (trade paper)
  1. Altars. 2. Household shrines. 3. Spiritual life—Christianity. I. Title.
   BV195.G75 2004
   249—dc22   2004014148

10 9 8 7 6 5 4 3 2 1

ISBN 1-55725-402-8

Published by Paraclete Press
Brewster, Massachusetts
www.paracletepress.com
Printed in the United States of America.

Contents

To
Winnie
with thanks for your
inspiration and faithfulness

INTRODUCTION

I like to rise early when I visit my family in Virginia on their Shenandoah Valley farm. I go sit on Bell's Ridge, where I can watch the sun rise over the Blue Ridge Mountains and smell the day come to life. Afterward I often set out to wander over the land, letting my soles lead me to whatever field or cranny they might find. Last summer, I headed down a wooded hillside I had never explored. I ducked under low growing cedars, stepped over downed trees, and pushed through brambles as I walked beside a huge gully that led down to the pit of a ravine. There at the very bottom, I discovered with amazement a gigantic, ancient oak tree.

I didn't think this timbered land had any such huge specimens still around; yet here, in a hidden hollow, stood a tree hundreds of years old with a history so much longer than my history. I walked all around it, looking from various angles at its gnarled roots, towering top, and wide breadth. Alone in the woods, I spoke out praise to the Creator, Who had grown and hidden this magnificent tree for so long, perhaps just so I might marvel on this morning at God's wondrous ways. I took an acorn from the oak, stuck it in my jacket pocket, and headed home, full of wonder and worship, reminiscent of the Magi who followed a star and found a babe in a manger.

I set the acorn, a sign of the grand grace of Creation that God gave to me that day, on a little table that sits in the corner of our family's cottage. The acorn joined a tiny bird's nest discovered on the ground on another morning walk; a little box containing one of my son's baby teeth, which fell out on a visit in Virginia but with all the other wonders of the day was never put under a pillow for the tooth fairy; a turtle's shell; a rock in the shape of a J for my son Josh; and a small notebook that can display quotes. The table that holds all these objects, set amidst our daily comings and goings, is our simple family altar. When I light a candle there and sit for quiet prayer, the tiny offerings remind me of God's great works and help my heart come to worship.

Altars were built by the patriarchs as reminders of God's working and have been at the center of worship spaces in both the Jewish tabernacle and Christian churches throughout history. Yet I had not imagined altars for my own home worship until I saw a presentation by Winnie Honeywell, director of Family Life Ministry in the Diocese of Galveston-Houston ten years ago.

As a family therapist, I had been invited to speak on family of origin to a group of Family Life ministers, paid church staff, and volunteers who worked with families in a variety of capacities. Before I was introduced, the class conducted a worship ritual that they used to start each session. While playing music of special significance to her family, Honeywell slowly placed objects that represented God's presence in her family life on a small altar and then briefly explained their meaning. I was mesmerized by the power of this ritual, as it communicated God's holy presence in the midst of ordinary lives.

I went home and created an altar space for myself. I began to adopt the practice when I traveled, putting together a small pilgrim altar wherever I was staying. I began to study the use of altars in biblical history and in the traditions of the church. My own personal altar became so helpful in developing my attentiveness to God and cultivating an attitude of gratefulness that I began to teach this practice as part of a family spirituality class in my church. I introduced it when I taught contemplative spirituality on retreats. When I was asked to develop the family systems unit of the training for Community of Hope, a ministry that trains and supports lay chaplains within a variety of church parishes, I incorporated the family altar, which speaks louder than many words about God's presence in our everyday lives. The home altar is the most powerful way I know to help people become aware of God's unique presence in their history and ongoing journey. The time seems ripe to put on paper for others beyond my own community the workings and wonders, the stories and possibilities of this spiritual practice of creating personal altars.

A strong biblical and historical tradition of altars will provide the foundation for our adapting them for personal family use. The whys of altar making will be examined, looking at the purposes and benefits of altars. The hows of altar making will be explored, discussing practical possibilities and alternatives for creating an altar. Using altars to develop richer spiritual practices for a deeper faith life is the most important goal of this book.

In the first part of the book, the discussion moves from the past to the present and from traveling to being at home. Chapter 1 lays out the scriptural foundation for altar building and the historic use of altars by Jews and by Christians of Catholic, Orthodox, and Protestant faiths. Describing pilgrimages from the Middle Ages up through the travels of today's people of faith, Chapter 2 offers ideas for using altars to see and serve God as spiritual pilgrims in the world. Chapter 3 focuses on two types of altars in the home: personal and family altars—and describes practical steps to create them and basic ways to use them.

The second part of the book focuses on the spiritual disciplines that the home altar supports. Ultimately an altar is not significant for how it appears as much as for how it is useful in the worship and devotional life of the user. The altar, like an icon, is meaningful in that it connects a person more personally with the living God. Chapters 4 and 5 introduce two historic spiritual disciplines, *lectio divina* and the *examen* of consciousness, and show how home altars enhance their practice. The final chapter issues a call to keep the faith and pass it on to the next generation by using altars for their most traditional purpose: remembrance and storytelling.

The final part of the book discusses additional possibilities for altar use. Chapter 7 explores outdoor altars, which can be especially conducive to personal renewal and inspiration. Chapter 8 introduces specific customs that revolve around altar use within several ethnic groups to encourage the use of altars to keep their faith heritage alive.

Equipped with the practical guidance provided in this book, you can begin using this simple but profoundly helpful spiritual tool in creative ways to further your personal awareness and worship of God. By offering a place to bring the fruit of our labors, the discoveries of our day, and our needs and challenges, the altar helps us live embodied lives of worship in ordinary time and space.

altars ancient and new

Altars have been meeting places between God and humans for ages and continue to be used in both old and new forms. In many ancient sites, rock piles intrigue visitors who can imagine the worship of their ancestors. In historic cathedrals around the world, centuries-old altars invite modern pilgrims to light candles in places where for generations believers have kept the light of Christ burning.

Though our modern altars may look somewhat different, the impulse to worship and to create a place in which to do that seems to be universal. Recently my sister visited the worksite of a friend and noticed the shelves in the cubicle workspace of the many workers there. Whether religious or not, their top shelf invariably was overflowing with personal items: pictures, children's artwork, plaques, small trinkets of remembrance. My friend Barbara, mother of three active children, has a favorite icon, a candle and her Bible beside her computer screen where she writes daily devotionals for her lay religious order.

The call of the God of the Bible is to worship in all times and places. Altars are a tangible way to designate a holy space and invite worship. So this section begins by looking at the practice of altar making in biblical times and the uses of altars throughout history. The next chapter introduces the attitude of pilgrimage which is essential for developing awareness of God, a heart attitude necessary for altar making. Moving from specific ways to use altars while traveling, the third chapter introduces essential practices and possibilities for using altars in everyday life at home.

Chapter One

Altars Through History: Meet with God

Build the altar of the LORD your God with fieldstones and
offer burnt offerings on it to the LORD your God.
Sacrifice fellowship offerings there, eating them and
rejoicing in the presence of the LORD your God.
And you shall write very clearly all the words of this law
on these stones you have set up.
—Deuteronomy 27:6-8

My friend John has a primitive brass oil lamp from the first century, found in the Galilean region of Israel. He imagines it might have burned in a shepherd's hut on a mountainside where Jesus prayed, or in a house along the lake while Jesus calmed the storm, or perhaps even on a table where Jesus shared a meal. John treasured the lamp for many years after receiving it as a gift on a pilgrimage to the Holy Land. He never lit the lamp lest it lose its dusty antique finish. However, when his wife, Betsy, was diagnosed with brain cancer, she asked if she could light it. Begrudgingly at first, he filled the lamp with olive oil and offered it to her to light. Betsy often spent time in those difficult days before a little home altar down in their basement. When her illness made it impossible for her to minister at the church where she worked, that altar became the place where she offered up her petitions and praises. In that dark, musty space in a home in Buffalo, New York, the old oil lamp shone brightly, bringing the light of Jesus into a family's dark journey with cancer.

Altars have long played a role in faith history and worship within homes. Since the time of our ancestors in faith, altars have been used as places for remembrance of God's works, for offerings of sacrifice and praise, and for listening to God's word. I hope that through this book, altars, like John's precious lamp, can be brought into current use to help the light of Christ shine brightly in all our homes.

The Biblical Tradition of Altar Use

One of the first stories of dramatic interchange between God and humans in history is that of the Flood. At the center point of resolution stands the first biblical account of altar building.

Since Creation, humans had multiplied on the earth, and if there had been newspapers in ancient times they would have been filled from front to back with reports of carousing, violent crimes, and warring factions. God considers wiping out the whole of humankind as a bad experiment in offering independence. Perhaps in section D in the back of those ancient newspapers would have been the only redeeming story, that of one man, Noah, who is so righteous that he is described as walking with God. Since the ears of his heart are open, he is able to hear God give him incredibly detailed instructions for building an ark 450 feet long, 75 feet wide, and 45 feet high to save himself and his family and all species of creatures.

A catastrophic flood covers the earth, destroying all of humankind except this little bobbling boat of believers who huddle together for forty days of torrential flooding and months of waiting for the waters to recede and the earth to dry. When finally Noah and his wife and his sons and his sons' wives come out of the ark, they do not go off exuberantly stretching their legs and exploring the new landscape. No, Genesis 8 records that first Noah builds an altar to the Lord and sacrifices offerings on it. The Lord is personally affected by this: "The LORD smelled the pleasing aroma and said in his heart: 'Never again will I curse the ground because of man'" (8:21). God goes on to make a profound promise to never again destroy all life with a flood and offers the rainbow as a sign of His covenant with Noah and his descendants.

The role of the altar in establishing a passionate, personal relationship between humans and God continues throughout biblical and worship history. At almost every point when God appears in the Bible, the patriarchs build an altar in the sacred spot of interchange with God. After the Lord asks Abram to leave the land of his birth and go forth, He appears to Abram in the new land of Canaan and says, "To your offspring I will give this land" (Genesis 12:7). So Abram builds an altar to the Lord. When God appears to Isaac one night at Beersheba and says, "I am the God of your father Abraham. Do not be afraid, for I am with you; I will bless you and will increase the number of your descendants for the sake of my servant Abraham" (Genesis 26:24-25), Isaac's first response is to build an altar there and call on the name of the Lord. When the Lord appears to Jacob in his dream about a ladder going up to heaven and a promise of God's presence with him and his descendants, Jacob takes the stone that had been under his head, sets it up as a pillar, and pours oil on it (Genesis 28:10–22). When he returns to Canaan years later in reconciliation with his brother, Esau, God tells him to go back to Bethel, settle there, and build an altar to God. Jacob builds the altar and commands all his people to get rid of foreign gods, and worship God there (Genesis 35:1–7). In these narratives, the act of building an altar after a powerful experience of God, to sanctify the place as well as to offer worship, seems a natural impulse from the heart.

Altars also arose historically to commemorate great works of God. After the battle of the Israelites and the Amalekites, in which Moses held up his hands until the Israelites won, the Lord asks Moses to write the story on a scroll to be remembered. Moses then builds an altar and calls it "The LORD is my Banner" (Exodus 17:15). Later, when the Israelites finally cross the Jordan River to enter the Promised Land, Joshua carefully follows the exhortation that Moses gave him: "Build the altar of the LORD your God with fieldstones and offer burnt offerings on it to the LORD your God. Sacrifice fellowship offerings there, eating them and rejoicing in the presence of the LORD your God. And you shall write very clearly all the words of this law on these stones you have set up" (Deuteronomy 27:5–8; Joshua 8:30–35). In both instances, the altar was constructed to serve as a means of remembering God's powerful work in the lives of the faithful. The altars of Moses and Joshua stand as models for altars today as places of remembrance.

Beyond declaring God's appearance or mighty works, altars have also had an ongoing role as places where God and God's people can meet. God gives the first detailed command regarding altar building after delivering the Ten Commandments and before putting forth the laws that Moses will set before the Hebrews. Exodus 20:23–25a records God as saying "Do not make any gods to be alongside me; do not make for yourselves gods of silver or gods of gold. Make an altar of earth for me and sacrifice on it your burnt offerings and fellowship offerings, your sheep and goats and your cattle. Wherever I cause my name to be honored, I will come to you and bless you. If you make an altar of stones for me, do not build it with dressed stones. . . . " Altars have been and continue to be built through history by all peoples to all variety of gods. What differentiates biblical altars is their dedication to the worship of the one living creator God, Yahweh. Items placed on the altar are not items to be worshipped in and of themselves but rather are an offering of worship or thanks to the one holy God.

Moses goes on to describe God's specific details for building of the tabernacle, where God promised to dwell with the Jewish people. God gives exact instructions for the tabernacle, which includes two altars that have had a place in the various temples of the Jewish people for centuries. The altar of burnt offering stood in a courtyard outside the tent over the tabernacle as a place where various offerings were given according to the law (Exodus 27). The smaller altar of incense, or golden altar, stood inside the tabernacle in what was called the Holy Place (Exodus 30). Morning and evening services began with the high priest offering incense on this altar as a type of prayer. Once a year, on the Day of Atonement, the blood of the sin offering was put on the four projections of this altar, known as the horns.

For Christians, Christ's death upon the cross is considered the once-and-forever perfect sacrifice upon the altar of burnt offering and final atonement for sins, making daily and yearly sacrifices of blood no longer necessary. The writer of the letter to the Hebrews elaborates on the Jewish practice of making offerings for atonement and the role of Christ: "How much more, then, will the blood of Christ, who through the eternal Spirit offered himself unblemished to God, cleanse our consciences from acts that lead to death, so that we may serve the living God!" (Hebrews 9:14). The first letter of John also explains this clearly: "[Jesus] is the atoning sacrifice for our sins, and not only for ours but also for the sins of the whole world" (1 John 2:2; see also 4:10).[1] As the high priest offered incense on the altar on behalf of the people of faith, Christ is the great high priest ever interceding on our behalf: "Now there have been many of those priests, since death prevented them from continuing in office; but because Jesus lives forever, he has a permanent priesthood. Therefore he is able to save completely those who come to God through him, because he always lives to intercede for them" (Hebrews 7:23–25). The believers' role is to continue to offer a sacrifice of praise to God through Jesus (Hebrews 13:15).

Not only central in worshippers' lives on earth, the altar also has a central place in heaven, as viewed in the vision in Revelation: "Another angel, who had a golden censer, came and stood at the altar. He was given much incense to offer, with the prayers of all the saints, on the golden altar before the throne" (Revelation 8:3). Thus, from the sacrifice of Christ and into the final offerings of praise in eternity, the altars of the temple in early Jewish history continue to have a place in Christian worship.

Altars in the History of Christian Worship

Altars have been present in Christian worship since the beginnings of Christianity. The early Christians often worshipped in homes, where the altar was probably a simple table around which the faithful gathered. St. Paul distinguishes between the altars for the worship of pagan gods and of Christ the Lord. "You cannot have a part in both the Lord's table and the table of demons" (1 Corinthians 10:21). When Christians were forced to hide and worship in catacombs, the altar was sometimes a coffin, out of necessity. This practice was most likely the precursor of the tradition in some Catholic and Orthodox churches of building altars with a reliquary to hold relics of saints. Throughout the centuries the sanctuaries of most Christian churches have been built with a central high altar in front, especially in the Roman Catholic, Orthodox, Anglican, Episcopal, Lutheran, and other highly liturgical denominations. In some Catholic and Orthodox churches, elaborate procedures for dressing the altar and placing the vessels on it are part of the preparation for worship. Most altars hold candles as symbols of the light of Christ, as well as a Bible, symbolizing the sacred Word of God to the people. In Protestant churches a simpler table without adornment is more often used.

From the time of the early Christians, the altar has served as the place where the Eucharistic bread and wine are prepared. Representatives of the people, during the offertory in many liturgical churches, bring forward to the altar, bread and wine to be consecrated for the Eucharist as well as the monetary offerings of the congregation. As the bread and wine are being prepared, believers also offer thanks and rededicate themselves to Christ. The Episcopal liturgy asks God to accept "our sacrifice of praise and thanksgiving" as worshippers go on to "offer and present unto thee, O Lord, our selves, our souls and bodies, to be a reasonable, holy, and living sacrifice unto thee."[2] The altar is the place where worshippers bring all that they have—bread, possessions, and self—to God. After consecration, the gifts of bread and wine, the body and blood of Christ, are offered back as the gifts of God to the people of God.

While altars are central in the worship of Christian communities, smaller personal altars have an important role and long tradition in worship as well, though it is less well-known. In rural parts of medieval Europe, Christians who could not easily travel to church for community worship used home altars for worship.[3] When immigrants first came to the United States, they often worshipped around home altars before they were able to build churches.[4] In nineteenth-century Mexico, as legislation sought to separate church and state, home altars sprang up and became a more central part of devotional life. These Mexican home altars frequently included *retablos*, or sacred images painted on tin, as well as flowers, novenas, and rosaries.[5] This tradition was passed on through generations of Mexican families and brought to Texas by Hispanic immigrants. Catholic believers from a variety of backgrounds today are familiar with the idea of a home altar of some sort because they observed their grandparents or parents faithfully reciting the rosary in a prayer space. In the Orthodox tradition, families have small home altars, often with icons. In fact, each member of the family may have his or her own little sacred space with candles, a cross, and an icon of his or her own patron saint.

Within Protestant communities, emphasis is not on the assembly of a home altar but on the importance of the home altar as a way of worship. The General Assembly of the Presbyterian Church in the United States, in a "Pastoral Letter on Family Religion" in 1909, stated, "The family altar is the determining factor in the security, perpetuity, and efficiency of family life. Family worship is a test of the faith of parents and the reality of religion. It is the union of precept and example in the instruction of children."[6] In the current *Orthodox Presbyterian Book of Church Order*, families are instructed to prepare for public Communion at the "family altar" by "reading the Scriptures, by holy meditation, and by prayer, especially for a blessing upon the ministry of the Word."[7] Ideas for the "family altar"—meaning worship and devotions gathered as a family in the home—are also current in Protestant literature.

In the biblical accounts of Noah and the patriarchs and throughout the history of Christian worship, altars serve a central role. They provide a way to openly declare allegiance to God, proclaim God's glorious works, offer thanksgiving, and call believers to ongoing worship. If they serve such a vital role in the history of the faith, certainly their use in our personal faith lives can enhance our everyday wonder and worship of God.

CHAPTER TWO

Pilgrim Altars:
Go with God

"You like it? It's yours. Take it with you."
Guide Kenny taught us how to make soul finds,
so we gathered gifts throughout the Holy Land
to store within our pockets, hearts, and minds.

In Galilee, we made pilgrim pictures of the sunset sea,
scooped pottery pieces from Solomon's ancient mounds,
heard Yuval's beach search story with it rainbow find,
realized milk and honey flow from different grounds.

We pray we will not pass like Dead Sea pilgrims,
where living water fills with nothing flowing out,
but will take our collected traveling treasures
to grow within and share with others all about.

—Take It with You[1]

Noah, Abram, Isaac, Jacob, and Joshua all built their altars to a God whom they encountered powerfully along their life's journey. The saints who established the Christian church, Peter while fishing and Paul along the road to Damascus also first met Jesus in everyday encounters. If the primary purpose of an altar is to be a meeting place with God, the attitude of looking for God must be the beginning practice for altar making. This starts spiritually in cultivating a pilgrim heart, whether traveling far away or staying at home. Simple personal altars can then be places to gather representations of God's presence through our days.

I was introduced to the idea of pilgrimage when I had the opportunity to take a trip to the Holy Land with my son Ben when he was twelve years old. Before we left, I saw my pastor in passing at Sunday service. He paused, looked at me with great intensity, and told me there was one thing I must not forget: "Be sure to make it a pilgrimage." What did he mean by that, I wondered? I knew of pilgrims in the Middle Ages, but how as a modern traveler was I to make a pilgrimage? How was a pilgrimage different from a trip?

I pondered these questions as I traveled, and I began to realize that a pilgrimage has less to do with where you are going and everything to do with your attitude toward the journey. The heart of pilgrimage is going with God and being open to the leading of the Spirit. The pilgrim rarely has the schedule all mapped out. Even when a careful plan has been developed, as must happen when the travel involves a large group, pilgrims expect that the important moments of the journey will be revealed along the way. A pilgrim allows time for seeing with the heart, stopping when the Spirit blows in a particular place or person, and modifying the journey according to the leadings of the moment.

The best guidance Ben and I received for our pilgrimage came from the youngest member of our family. Our plan was to leave early in the morning, so the night before I sat down with my son Andrew, who was four at the time, to say good-bye. I told him I would like to pray for him and asked if he would pray for us. I prayed a long and flowery prayer that we have long since forgotten. Then he prayed. "Dear Lord, I pray they may see Jesus wherever they go. Amen." I was dumbstruck by the simplicity and depth of this four-year-old's prayer. We used it as our anchor throughout the trip, often asking each other, "Where did you see Jesus today?"

The places where we saw Jesus were often in the little discoveries along the way or the lessons that ordinary people taught us. We learned about God's generosity from our guide who told us that at age six his mother asked him to give away half his clothes for the Jews coming in as refugees. We saw God's hospitality as our guide picked up an Israeli soldier hitchhiker for part of our journey. The delicious oranges from the roadside stand were the sweetness of creation for us.

The holiest item Ben and I brought home from our trip was something ordinary we had taken with us that was changed by being there. We arrived at the Church of the Nativity in Bethlehem on January 6, unbeknownst to us the Orthodox day for celebrating the birth of Christ. Our driver was upset because it meant more traffic, but I was thrilled, grateful for God's good planning that was beyond my knowledge. We were able to duck into the tiny cave beneath the church, the site where tradition holds that Christ was born, before it was cordoned off from the crowds. On the ground was a gold star with a small well of oil in its center. Ben knelt quickly to pray, and his baseball cap fell off his head and landed in the oil. From then on, the cap with its scent of holy oil was his reminder of God's timing and presence with us on the trip.

Putting a small item representing the godly discoveries or a journal with writings about them on a little altar space wherever we are staying is a way to consciously acknowledge the faces and graces of God.

My first inspiration for using an altar to capture the sightings of God while traveling, came many years after the trip to the Holy Land when I was able to go to the home town of St. Francis of Assisi for a conference. I stayed at a local convent, and one of the women who also stayed there epitomized the pilgrim spirit.

I can still recall her vibrant sense of wonder when she arrived late to one of the conference's quiet lunches, breathless and with her hands full of gigantic yellow flowers that she had discovered in a little market. A few days later, on the day we were to leave, I experienced debilitating back pains and wondered how I would be able to make it home. This woman I barely knew invited me to her room so she could massage my back. As I lay under her tender ministry, I noticed her windowsill, filled with the small tokens of God's presence that she had collected, including the buoyant flowers, over her days in Assisi. She had learned to create a pilgrim altar of thanks wherever she traveled.

After seeing her altar, I began creating a small personal altar space—on a windowsill, a night table, or even a corner of a desk—whenever I traveled. My friend Betsy had a small collection of traveling icons that her husband graciously shared with her women friends after her death. When I travel, I place on my pilgrim altar the icon I have from her, which pictures Christ with a vine coming out of His side and wrapped around His shoulders. Fruit hangs down His other side, and He is squeezing it into a Communion cup. Gazing at this icon, I remember the Communion Christ offers to us wherever we go if we abide in Him. I add to my altar a small candle and travel-size Bible as well as small gifts that I find on my pilgrim journey, representations of my little holy sightings through the day. I might add a pine cone from an awesome tree discovered on a quiet walk, a ticket stub from a play that struck home, or a poignant word spoken by a stranger that I have scribbled on a scrap of paper. I have discovered that the real pilgrimage begins when I look for, and expect God in the unplanned moments of travel. And to remind myself of God's wondrous and redeeming work in these sacred moments, I place small tokens on my pilgrim altar.

The Purpose of a Pilgrim Altar

A pilgrim altar is a way to visibly acknowledge God as Lord of our lives and our travels. Our family has a habit of praying in the car before we leave for a trip, making clear our need for God's guidance and safety as well as our openness to God's presence along the way. A pilgrim altar is a tangible way to show our desire for God to be Lord of our journeying. An altar also creates a place to pray and give thanks at the end and beginning of each day, while offering a space to display signs of God's presence along the way.

Creating a Pilgrim Altar

A traveling altar can be as simple as a candle on a nightstand or as elaborate as a table set with a special cloth and adorned with beautiful objects in the center of the room. A candle and a travel Bible make a wonderful foundation for a pilgrim altar. My husband, who travels a great deal as part of his job, scoops up the leftover candles from the Easter Eve Vigil each year and uses them to create sacred space in his hotel rooms. Small travel candles sold by some companies are safe and easy to carry on a trip. A special icon or picture of a patron saint might be carried from home. Some people like to bring a picture of family members in a leather or plastic frame that does not break or that folds up easily for using on a pilgrim altar. Such a picture frame could also hold the picture of someone you are praying for. A simple cloth can also be carried for the altar.

Once you have a few simple objects from home, creating a pilgrim altar requires designating some small space in the place where you are staying. The beauty of such a space is the ability to convert wherever you are staying into a prayer space simply by virtue of a simple altar arrangement. I remember how such a transformation occurred at a conference my husband and I attended. During one session in the hotel's ballroom, Pastor Gordon McDonald began by saying, "I declare this a sanctuary." Spiritually, the massive room was turned into a worship space in an instant. In a similar way, by making an altar and praying there, we can turn a hotel suite, dingy motel room, hostel bed, or basement corner with a blowup mattress into personal sacred space.

The making of a pilgrim altar becomes a more creative process when you begin adding small items that represent signs of God's goodness to you during the day of travel—a pebble from the garden in a church where you prayed, a postcard of a piece of art that inspired you, a label from a bottle of water that quenched your thirst at the end of a long hike, or just a word that spoke strongly in a conversation that was scribbled on a napkin can be an offering of thanks and praise to God for graces along the way.

If you are traveling from place to place, the items for the altar can be put in a small cloth or plastic bag and spread out each time you arrive in a new place. In such a way, we designate that holiness has less to do with place than with our attitude and prayerfulness in it.

We can use a pilgrim altar to offer thanks to God for the pilgrimage experiences of the day, but we can also incorporate our pilgrim experiences into personal altars at home, reminding ourselves always to live as pilgrims. Our little items can be emptied onto our altars at home when we return, or just one item can be chosen as a token remembrance. Another way to bring pilgrim memories home is with pictures. I have, in addition to normal family photo albums, a pilgrim photo album, which includes photographs I have taken on pilgrimages, but not of the typical tourist sights. To anyone else, they might not seem remarkable or particularly photo-worthy. To me, however, these photos are scenes of the Holy Spirit's presence. A picture of pine cones on the tree outside the library in the Assisi convent where I stayed reminds me of a call to live a life that bears fruit. A picture of goat poop on a Bolivian hillside reminds me of the unusual leading that took me and a friend to an unexpected hilltop destination. With my pilgrim photo album, which is on my home altar, I am reminded of those moments when I felt so thankful for God's presence.

Cultivating a Pilgrim Attitude

Beyond the apparent purposes, the pilgrim altar serves the deeper spiritual purpose of helping to cultivate a pilgrim attitude. Key to developing a pilgrim attitude is what I call traveling by heart. By this, I mean learning to listen to the inner heart for guidance and direction rather than being controlled by the outer itinerary, appearance, or direction of others. This requires learning to pay attention to inner promptings and the moving of the Holy Spirit.

Practically, this is easiest without a tightly designated itinerary so there is plenty of time for listening and flexibility to go where and in the speed that the Spirit leads. Jesus said He did not have a set place to lay His head. During His ministry, He and His disciples would simply come to a town and find a willing host for whatever period of time God directed. True monastic pilgrims, such as the unnamed writer of *The Way of a Pilgrim* who describes the use of the simple repetitious prayer of the name of Jesus, also lived each day truly directed moment by moment by the Spirit's leading. Robert Wild in his book, *Waiting for the Presence,* describes his trip to the Holy Land as a pilgrim. He went with the intent of going to holy sites and waiting at each one for however long it took the Spirit's presence to come.

Few of us have the time or courage to travel so freely as a pilgrim. Yet any of us can adopt some aspects of a pilgrim attitude. Even with a set group schedule, we can walk more slowly, listen carefully for words from God, and look for signs of God's appearing along the way. The crucial recognition is that God's appointments are often not written clearly on the official itinerary. The most meaningful connections may come from people we meet along the way, from interactions that were not planned, and from things we see that were not the main event. On a recent trip, our group had planned to visit a harp factory. When we got to the street, we discovered the shop had moved; so instead we looked around the other stores. At one there were biblical dolls perfect for my niece and a prayer shawl hand-painted on silk. But the real gift was conversation with the shop owners, who it turns out had been bombed earlier and needed not only business but prayerful guests.

In the week prior to leaving for a trip to the Holy Land, my sister had a car accident. The woman who had backed into her got out frazzled and upset, but my sister looked at the minor damage and waved her on with forgiveness. As she got back in the car, she sensed God preparing her for the trip with the admonition to "Be aware of whom you bump into." The advice is pilgrim wisdom. She met a woman in an airport store who became an Israeli friend, who happened to work at the American Embassy. At the Church of the Holy Sepulcher, which commemorates where Jesus died, asking a simple question of a young monk from Ghana led to his leading my sister right into Jesus' tomb for time to pray there. Arriving home, she left her computer on the airplane; thankful for the man who helped retrieve it, she offered to pray for him. With grateful astonishment he told her of his mother with cancer who had just been given a few weeks to live. She has been linked prayerfully to so many because she is paying attention to the daily "bumping into" people.

Cultivating an attitude of remembrance is another way of traveling as a pilgrim and not as a tourist. My family came up with the idea of taking "pilgrim photos." The idea germinated years ago when my sister and I were riding horseback over my grandparents' farm in Virginia and came upon a gorgeous sunset. I said I wished I had a camera, and my sister replied, "Take a picture in your mind." Most of the pictures I have taken with a camera have been lost or are stored away in boxes somewhere, but I still have the pilgrim picture of that sunset, ready upon demand. When Ben and I went to Israel with the admonition to be pilgrims, he reinitiated the idea of savoring a beautiful scene in our minds and hearts rather than rushing for a camera. I remember standing on top of Mount Carmel and looking out over the sea as the sun was setting. I said, "Let me go get the camera for this!" As I was about to hurry down the hill to the car, Ben stopped me and said, "Mom, take a pilgrim photo." I stood there while the sun sank below the horizon, and even today I can easily bring up that scene in my memory, complete with the soft breeze and sparkling sun on the rippling water. The idea of taking mental pictures has apparently taken hold with Ben for good; when his girlfriend put together a photo album for him a number of years ago, on the back page she had a written list of "pilgrim photos." Traveling to a new place can help develop a pilgrim attitude because our routines are upset and we expect to meet new people and experience new situations. This heightened openness can be used to help us develop the pilgrim heart that we need for even our ordinary days. Simply by leaving comfortable surroundings, we have an opportunity to practice dependency on God. When we take a pilgrimage to a holy sight, the very sacredness of the soil and sights can heighten our awareness of God. Looking over the city of Jerusalem from the Mount of Olives, it is hard not to be stirred by this holy ground. Sitting in the massive St. Peter's Church in Rome with its ornate carvings of saints from history all around, one cannot help but imagine the hosts of saints who have gone before. Such a pilgrimage helps develop the attitude of wonder.

The attentiveness, on the other hand, required to transform a trip into a pilgrimage can be most difficult in the places that the world has deemed holiest, and perhaps my priest knew this when he admonished me before my trip to the Holy Land. Many designated holy places in the world are often now the most commercialized as well. Temple grounds remain places of merchandising and profiteering, just as they were when Jesus took a whip to chase the money-changers out. On our trip to the Holy Land we visited the Garden of Gethsemane, a place of such agony for Jesus on the day before His crucifixion. Between the crowds and the conversations of the many visitors, it took some discipline to kneel and simply sit in that sacred space. As we were leaving, we were barraged by a man trying to sell us the tacky religious trinkets displayed on top of his old car. At one point he asked, "Anybody want more Jesus?" Yes, I thought, but

I will need to work hard to look past you and your things to keep a still heart that is open to finding Jesus.

Maintaining a pilgrim spirit was also a struggle for me in Assisi. I had imagined going to this holy place, where the saint himself had walked, to find spiritual peace. And I did find it. But it took a lot of hard work to walk slowly, to not be caught up in the touristy invitations and shopping bargains. The group I was with stayed in a convent amidst Assisi's peaceful pebbled lanes and tolling bells, but we needed earplugs for the nightly noises of partying and music at nearby clubs. The plaza outside the sacred church where St. Francis heard God's call to him was full of vendors selling plastic flowers, cheap crosses, and ice cream cones. In order to walk in the peaceful aspect of Assisi rather than its current, busy ways, required concentrated resolution.

However difficult the experience might be, traveling to a place where we have to fight distractions prepares us for our real lives, which are full of demands and in which we are also called to walk as pilgrims. In Jesus' day, the temple was full of vendors, yet He called His disciples to come and follow Him. Our lives everyday are part of the greater pilgrimage from earth to heaven, as John Bunyan portrays so well in his classic *Pilgrim's Progress*. The challenges are not simply or primarily physical ones but rather are spiritual challenges as we encounter earthly situations.

Although it took a trip to the Holy Land for me to understand the Christian call to pilgrimage, I have since realized that any trip away from home can offer the possibility of pilgrimage if we determine to pay particular attention to God wherever we walk. My husband's job at an airline has afforded me wonderful opportunities to visit known holy places, but I have just as often experienced spiritual pilgrimage in short journeys closer to home.

I learned about simple spiritual pilgrimage most poignantly on a trip with Betsy's daughter, Shemaleiah. She and I had plans to go to France. She would fly from Buffalo to Newark, where we would meet and catch our plane to Paris. The evening we were to leave, all the planes out of Buffalo were snowed in, and so she was unable to get to Newark for our flight to Paris. Because of the timing we would not be able to reschedule our trip. Sitting in the Newark airport with my careful plans bungled, I wondered what we could possibly do. Then I remembered a little convent just an hour away, where Betsy, as my spiritual director, had suggested long ago I visit for my first experience of a silent retreat. I called Shemaleiah and proposed the idea of visiting the convent instead. Again I heard wisdom from youth: "Anne, that's fine," she said. "What's most important is that we have time together." The sisters at the convent were willing to welcome us, so suddenly a new plan took shape. When Shemaleiah arrived late that night in Newark, we took a bus with many other delayed passengers to get a rental car. A woman asked what our story was, and we said contentedly that we were supposed to go to Paris but had to change our plans and would be spending our time at a convent in New Jersey. This certainly sounded strange but was indeed God's graced plan.

The trip turned out better than an exhausting trip abroad might have, as it allowed us both to enjoy some needed rest and quiet at an emotionally charged time. Our pilgrimage was more of an inner journey, in which we explored our grief and sensed God's gracious companionship. The rich soil we walked on in our own souls and on the grounds of that convent produced poetry we would never have had time to write amidst a busy trip to a foreign place. The simple gifts of daisies on the table at dinner, a deer grazing in the cemetery, a giant pine tree outside the chapel window, and sleep for tired bodies were as lovely as anything France could have offered. I wrote a poem about the experience several days later.

PILGRIMAGE
Unless the Lord builds the house,
we read at vespers,
the builders labor in vain.

I planned a trip to France,
but we landed in New Jersey
at a convent saying prayers.

We discovered at our table
her mother's favorite daisies
in a vase my holy blue.

Looking out the chapel window
I saw pines with hanging cones,
like my Assisi sacred view.

I may have labored some in vain,
but the Builder of this trip
planned every detail for our hearts.

Using Altars on Group Pilgrimages

The pilgrim attitude can be cultivated intentionally when a whole group travels together and makes this a clear purpose. Rather than approaching the trip like typical tourists, the leader can allow time for reflection and develop a regular use of a group pilgrim altar with group devotions. I had the opportunity to help turn a church trip into a pilgrimage several years ago when the children's choir at our church took a trip to England.

The children who had sung in the choir for many years and were about to complete their time as choristers were offered the opportunity, along with many of their parents, to visit the places in England for which their choirs were named, Chichester and Canterbury. They would be singing at several events, including a Taizé service in a small-town church, a private Communion in Chichester Cathedral, and Evensong in Canterbury Cathedral. The leaders planned fun activities mixed with choir practices and services.

We developed a journal for the trip that included each day's itinerary, quotes, and white space for writing during the trip. At the beginning we wrote:

> We are embarking on an adventure, traveling to an ancient land and meeting new friends, eating different foods, and experiencing wondrous new things. We are not going as tourists. Instead, we are deliberately traveling in community from one holy place to another, offering the gift of our talents to the people of England and, more important, back to the One who has given us all things. Just as we will keep our physical sense open to discover the beauty of our new surroundings, we must also open the eyes of our hearts to discover the spiritual journey toward the sacred. We are going on pilgrimage: a physical journey that is, at its heart, an inward journey to God.

The trip began not on the bus or at the airport but with a commissioning service in our church, before we loaded the bus, which focused on the call to pilgrimage. We formed our first pilgrim altar there, spreading out our plain white pilgrim altar cloth and lighting our pilgrim candle, a large white candle that had been decorated with a Canterbury Cross and "Pilgrimage 2001" written using liquid wax. Over the next ten days, we would carry a wooden pilgrim cross as well as this cloth and candle as the foundation for our pilgrim altar in each place. I reminded the group that pilgrimage is not so much about going somewhere to see a sight. Pilgrimage is about walking with Jesus to be formed in Him and for Him. I invited all those present to bring with them not only their clothes, toiletries, and passports but also an open heart. We would use the trip to practice opening the eyes of our hearts, which St. Benedict said was the essential Christian discipline. The group then prayed from Ephesians 1:18-19 that the "eyes of your heart may be enlightened in order that you may know the hope to which he has called you, the riches of his glorious inheritance in the saints, and his incomparably great power for us who believe."

At our first stop in England, each pilgrim wrote his or her name and drew a symbol on the edge of the altar cloth as a visible sign of our community together. I then taught the group the practice of *lectio divina* (see Chapter 4 for a more detailed description of this spiritual practice), in which a Scripture passage is read slowly as listeners wait to hear the particular word or phrase that God quickens to them. After the reading, time is given for each person to repeat and meditate on his or her word or phrase.

In England, we began each morning with *lectio divina*, tuning our hearts' ears to God. Each evening we gathered as a community to reflect on the day's journey. I asked everyone to consider at what moment they felt closest to Jesus that day (see Chapter 5 for more details on the process of an evening *examen* of consciousness). After a time for personal reflection, we invited various pilgrims to share their moment and to write a word or draw a picture on the community altar cloth that represented it. The sharing together encouraged everyone to pay attention to God through the day and to realize how varied our experiences were. While some saw God in the face of a stranger or in the voices of children, others saw God in a flower or a piece of stone or the bells of a church. We brought our altar cloth with us wherever we went, spreading it on tables in retreat centers, on the grass of a courtyard, and on the altar of a school chapel. Wherever we gathered, these experiences of sharing centered us and reminded us of our calling as pilgrims and of the ways we had already experienced God. As our pilgrimage continued, our altar cloth became filled with a variety of images in many colors and revealed to all who saw it how we had experienced the presence of God along our way. The leaders also provided for the journey a small napkin to each individual for use as his or her own personal altar cloth, and upon which each person could write or draw daily discoveries. Once the trip was over, some of these napkins became personal altar cloths for the participants' altars at home. The candle was circulated over time to various pilgrims who were ill or in need in the months and years after the pilgrimage.

A group altar can be a way to powerfully connect the members of the group and to connect the group with God. Several years ago, I participated in a spiritual retreat with the Shalem Institute in Maryland. During the retreat, participants gathered for communal silent meditation around a large circular table. The table was covered with a simple white cloth, and a lit candle sat in the center of it. Without any specific encouragement to do so, people began setting small items on this community altar over the course of our days together. Little items—a sprig of holly, a word from Scripture, a red rock, a poem, a picture symbolizing a spiritual awakening—slowly gathered until by the end our altar was gently filled, like our own souls, with God's goodness.

When I offer retreats, I usually place an altar at the front of the room and use it to make the experience a sort of pilgrimage for everyone involved. I will frequently ask participants on the first night of the retreat to write a prayer for our time together and place it on the altar. Over the course of the retreat, I may also ask participants to place the "fruit" from various exercises on the altar: a word that captures the essence of God's calling or a poem that expresses personal grief or an image of a particular grace. Placing such items on the altar both for sanctifying and to give thanks is a physical way to offer them to God.

A group pilgrimage need not be a time just for remembering the group's needs and intentions. Before beginning a pilgrimage, we might determine to pray for a particular person or situation in the world as we travel. Because a pilgrimage affords us more time to be attentive to God, we can pray in special ways for the particular needs of others. This keeps us from focusing too much on ourselves and our group and reminds us of our interconnectedness with the rest of the body of Christ and of the world. On the church trip to England I took with the choirs, we visited a number of local churches or cathedrals, where there was always an opportunity to light a candle in petition. My friend Becky's husband had died just days before our pilgrimage, so I lit candles at churches we visited as an offering for her and her children, remembering their grief amidst the joy of our group of singing children. A name or symbol of a person being prayed for on a trip can be placed on the pilgrim altar as a reminder to lift him or her up often in prayer.

Being a Pilgrim at Home

While the opportunity to take a pilgrimage to a holy land is wonderful, our travels are often more routine. Ordinary business trips, family visits over holidays, or simple vacations may not seem like opportunities for pilgrimage. Yet with an open attitude, we can take on a pilgrim spirit in these travels too.

We actually don't have to travel far or even outside our own communities to experience a pilgrimage. A quiet walk in the woods, time in a local library, or prayer in the church chapel can become a pilgrim experience. Julia Cameron, in *The Artist's Way*, suggests a weekly artist date with one's own creative self.[2] Approaching such an outing with a pilgrim attitude might turn time in a bookstore, art center, museum, or nearby creek into a mini-pilgrimage.

As David Rensberger writes in *Itinerant Every Day*: "The key to everyday itinerancy is recognizing that each step on the obvious journeys, on the daily round and the lifelong adventure, is also a step on the secret one. . . . What our impatient, self-determined selves take for interruption and delay, the soul of the itinerant knows as God-given new direction, a shortcut to an appointment we didn't know we had. . . . By abandoning our predetermined destinations, we open ourselves to genuine traveling."[3]

You don't have to travel far or even outside your own community to experience a pilgrimage. Another way to practice pilgrimage at home is to walk a labyrinth. In the Middle Ages, people were known for taking long pilgrimages to the Holy Land. Many people, however, were unable to travel, so they found a way to journey at home by developing the labyrinth. One of the best known labyrinths is the one built into the floor of the cathedral in Chartres. The path within of concentric circles weaves in and about on its way to the center and back. Through the labyrinth, walkers open themselves to some of the same experiences that pilgrims on longer journeys enjoy. Labyrinth walkers take a physical journey, but the real journey, as with any pilgrimage, happens within the soul landscape. The labyrinth models our lives: the twists and turns of the path move us closer to and farther from the center, just as the twists and turns of life move us toward and away from our central call. In some ways, not having the external distractions that a faraway pilgrimage site might have, can make the labyrinth an even more powerful pilgrimage. Today many churches and retreat centers have labyrinths or hold periodic labyrinth walks on portable labyrinths set up for a day or evening. If you can locate a labyrinth in your community, you can experience pilgrimage as you journey with your feet and also with your heart.

As we don't have to travel to a faraway place to go on a pilgrimage, we don't have to always build our own pilgrim altars to have personal worship spaces when we travel. Many communities offer places prepared especially for pilgrims that encourage them to be still and experience God's presence.

Wherever I have lived, I have sought out a park, retreat center, convent, or monastery where small sanctuaries for worship have already been created. In my hometown of Houston, I have found Villa de Matel, the motherhouse of the Sisters of Charity of the Incarnate Word, to be my pilgrim oasis. There, an icon room has small partitioned spaces, each with a comfortable seat facing a different icon where individuals can light a candle and reflect. A listening room has similarly divided spaces, but its comfortable chairs facing windows that look out on the house's gardens, are equipped with headphones and a player for music or teaching tapes. When I visit my twin sister in Los Angeles, as I have done more frequently since her diagnosis with cancer, we often slip away to the gardens at Mater Dolorosa, a retreat center run by the Passionist fathers.

Often a particular corner at a retreat house or in a park will speak to me and become a place for my own pilgrim altar of sorts. If the space is indoors, I might arrange a chair for a special view out the window and light the same candle each morning. If the space is outdoors, I might designate God's quiet appearing or offer a personal thanksgiving by leaving a small rock, leaf, or twigs placed in the shape of a cross at a place in the woods.

It's not necessary to even leave our home to experience a pilgrimage. A small amount of private time, an afternoon, or a day set aside can be used as a small pilgrimage if we use that time to try to be more alert to God's guiding us through the day. This is not unlike taking time out from a tennis game to practice our serve or repeating a small portion of a piece of music at a slow speed before returning to the full piece at full speed. A planned time of solitude, without the many distractions of daily life, can open us more fully to God's presence and call. Such a pilgrimage is primarily a journey over the inner landscape, and the role of the pilgrim altar is to mark any particular awareness of God.

As we have learned to walk with a pilgrim attitude, through large or small trips, abroad or at home, we have eyes alert to see Jesus wherever we go. We use a pilgrim altar to remind us of God's presence along our way and as a place to offer thanks for the ways in which God appears. We need to bring this attitude of noticing and worshipping God along the paths of our lives into the ordinary spaces of our daily routines. This will serve us well as we turn to developing altars at home.

CHAPTER THREE

Home Altars:
Bring God Home

*Hear, O Israel: The LORD our God, the LORD is one.
Love the LORD your God with all your heart and with all
your soul and with all your strength. These commandments
that I give you today are to be upon your hearts. Impress
them on your children. Talk about them when you sit at
home and when you walk along the road, when you lie
down and when you get up. Tie them as symbols on your
hands and bind them on your foreheads. Write them on the
doorframes of your houses and on your gates.
—Deuteronomy 6:4–9*

Though the patriarchs did a lot of wandering and worshipping
as they went, they eventually landed in the place that would be
home. There they built altars that declared their allegiance to
God and established a regular place for prayer. Abraham built

an altar when he arrived at Shechem in Canaan, where God declared that he and his descendents would live. Jacob built an altar when he returned home to Bethel after running from his brother, Esau. Joshua built an altar when he crossed the Jordan with the Jews to finally enter the Promised Land. The judge Samuel, who traveled widely in his job, "always went back to Ramah, where his home was. . . . And he built an altar there to the LORD" (1 Samuel 7:15–17).

The first forms of altars for Jewish worship were those in the tabernacle and the temple. After the temple was destroyed and the Jews were dispersed, they began to consider their homes little sanctuaries, or *mikdash me'at*. Still today, the Jewish home is regarded as a place for worship and for remembering God's presence and great works. Many Jews designate the sanctity of their homes by placing on their doorposts a *mezuzah*, a small capsule that holds a scroll bearing the words of Deuteronomy 6:4–9 and 11:13–21. These passages command parents to teach the commandments of God to their children throughout all the activities and places of daily life and to place the words of God on their doorposts. The holiest day of the year, after the Day of Atonement, is every *Shabbat*, the Sabbath, which begins with the family gathered around a table to light candles, pray, share the *hallah*, and eat together. On Passover, a central day of remembrance, Jewish families cleanse their homes and prepare the *seder,* the commemorative service that is celebrated around the family dinner table. Thus, the tables of Jewish families are their most basic worship altars.

In the early years after Christ's death, Christians also gathered around their home tables for worship, breaking the bread and drinking the wine in remembrance of Jesus' last Passover *seder* with them before His death and resurrection. Before Christianity became widespread, homes were the main gathering places of the faithful. Today, in places where Christians are persecuted, the home continues to thrive as a place of worship.

In places where Christian worship takes place primarily within the church, families of various denominations maintain the tradition of worship in the home with the home altar. Some Roman Catholic homes have places for images of patron saints, candles, and designated prayers on a small altar or shelf or on the walls. In the Orthodox tradition every home must have an altar, as the home is considered to be "the little church." Orthodox homes are filled with icon corners as symbols of the family's faith, and prayers are incorporated into every aspect of life. Within the Protestant tradition, with its emphasis on biblical authority and the priesthood of all believers, everyone in the family is encouraged to make time for daily Bible readings and prayer.

By building an altar, we sanctify a space for worship. Often that is in a sanctuary for community worship. But our worship of God is not intended to be limited to or even primarily consist of corporate worship. Rather, in all times and places, we are called to acknowledge and give thanks to God. Fleshy, down-to-earth creatures that we are, we need tangible aids that help us remember to see and to praise God in our ordinary spaces of life. The home altar, serving the same purpose as those first altars by the patriarchs which declared their commitment to God of their lives and their territory, offers a way to set our homes apart as dedicated to God.

Personal Altars

Within the home, personal altars are those built for an individual's private devotions. Wherever we choose to worship on a daily or regular basis, we can set up a small altar to designate the space as sacred and provide a place for reminders of God. Even when other members of the family do not pray regularly, those persons whose worship of God is central in their lives can create a small place in their home that indicates their daily dedication to God. There each individual can cultivate their own personal love relationship with God.

Purposes of Personal Altars

The first purpose of a personal altar is to make a visible statement about a person's dedication to God. This symbolic value is significant in and of itself, like the *mezuzah* on the doorframe of a Jewish home. Within the Jewish and Christian tradition, altars are not built to be objects of worship, nor places to put objects of worship. The first of the great commandments is to worship God and have no other gods. Throughout both Old and New Testaments, believers are repeatedly reminded to turn from pagan gods and idols and worship God alone, the Creator of all life and the giver of all good gifts.

The home altar acts as a portal to God. Icons, similarly, are carefully created to point the praying person to God rather than in any way to be God themselves. So an altar is only a tool used to invite and enhance the worship of God. Its design needs always to be an aid to thanksgiving and worship, not an art object or design center in itself. Christian or Jewish altars are not destinations but rather trail markers pointing the heart on its way to God.

The second purpose of an altar is for active worship and spiritual growth. As a flame draws moths, a personal altar can help draw believers to prayer and worship, both on a regular basis and during difficult times. Its presence in the home alone can increase a person's awareness of God and his or her attitude of always seeking God's presence. That attitude is further cultivated when we build routines of prayer into our home lives, setting aside a time for prayer at the personal altar. The more we experience God's particular presence in those times of prayer at the altar, the more we identify it as a place of encountering God. Just coming to that place, we anticipate the comfort of God's presence, which has been felt there so many times before. When I sink into the familiar chair in front of my personal altar, light the candle there that was given to me by my sister, and glance at the icon from my late friend, I sink as well into a familiar and quiet spiritual space, which releases the worries that filled my mind just moments ago while I was climbing the stairs to my room. I sense the presence of God as well as the communion of the saints whom I know.

If you practice meditation or centering prayer, in which you seek to quiet your soul from outer and inner distractions to just sit in the presence of God, a regular prayer space is particularly helpful. By coming to the same place each time, the reservoir of spiritual memories can help you enter more easily into a sense of God's presence.[1] When I find myself in the middle of a dry spiritual season or a tough time, the items I have chosen for my altar stand as reminders of a God who has indeed been present to me and who has personally worked in my life. Even when prayer is difficult or impossible, simply being at our personal altar is a way of praying. One friend of mine suffered from a long bout of pneumonia several years ago and did not have the energy even to pray. All she could do was light a candle and sit in front of her altar, and that was prayer enough for that season.

Each person's altar place can become his or her own monastic pew or cell, as it were, his or her own place for returning to God and following devotional calls. Whatever the place and whatever items or images we set there, they become testimony to God's personal love relationship with each one of us.

Creating a Personal Altar

The personal altar, like an icon, should point the praying person to God. Its design needs always to facilitate thanksgiving and worship, not to be something to worship in itself. In the same way that altars in churches vary—from elaborate high altars with gold candlesticks and seasonal altar cloths to a small table covered with a plain white cloth and holding a simple wooden cross—altars in homes are as different as the people they serve. And because home altars do not have to follow church specifications, the user is free to think creatively when setting up his or her personal altar.

Place. The first question to ask in creating a personal altar is where it should be placed. If your primary purpose is to dedicate your home and remind yourself of God whenever you enter, placing the altar at the entryway can be useful. If you wish to make the altar central to your whole living space, putting it in the living room can make it easily visible to you as well as to guests. Often the best place for a personal altar is the place where you are most comfortable spending time praying or in personal devotion. That might be in your bedroom or in a corner chair of the den, or perhaps at the kitchen table. Choosing a place that will be seen and used regularly is more important than having a place that looks beautiful. I find that placing my altar where I can easily see it from the chair where I pray is helpful, and if I can reach it also to write in a journal or place a new object or word on the altar, even better. Some people actually have a prayer bench with kneeler and shelf that is made for personal prayer.

If a larger space in the home is available, such as an extra room, closet, or bathroom, it can be dedicated for prayer and worship, with not only an altar but also places for kneeling or sitting and with objects decorating the walls. A priest I know has built a little chapel in his basement that he uses for his own personal prayer, and he also invites guests to use it when they come for a personal retreat.

Form. Tables are traditionally used for altars in the home, though the size and type of table can vary tremendously. A small table that has been handed down through the family, has been carefully chosen by a family member, or has been built by a woodcrafter in the family can add to the sense of preciousness of the altar. Some companies manufacture home altars that are a bit more ornate and are designed to be special centerpieces for the home.[2] Yet any form of table will do, especially because it is likely to be covered with a cloth. An upside-down crate, a TV tray, or an end table can serve perfectly well.

If there is limited space in the home, a shelf on a bookcase or on a wall can be used, especially if the user prefers to look at it instead of kneel or sit in front of it. A shelf tends to be more common for personal altar spaces in a bedroom. Occasionally a niche in a wall is made into a little altar or shrine, especially if the believer is Catholic or Orthodox and has a patron saint.

Cloth. Historically, most church altars have altar cloths, so we can incorporate the tradition in our personal home altars as well. While a simple white cloth will do, we can also borrow from various faith traditions to come up with a creative altar cloth. For instance, in liturgical churches, the particular colors and styles of the cloth are determined by the season in the church year. In Orthodox churches, the "vesting" of the altar is a symbolic and careful process. Those who follow the church year closely in their personal worship may wish to alternate colored cloths, or at least colored runners, on their personal altars according to the season. We can also choose a cloth for its personal significance or create our own cloth. One woman I know chose a piece of lace crocheted by her grandmother, who had been the pillar of faith in the family. A quilter could make a small altar cloth with a biblical motif. A knitter of prayer shawls might well want to knit an altar cloth and possibly attach a piece of fringe for each shawl given away.[3]

Another creative approach is to take a plain piece of cloth and decorate it in a way that indicates your own sense of yourself as created and called by God. In one workshop I offered, I asked participants to think of the times in their lives when they felt they were most fully living their calling in Christ. Afterward, they chose a word or symbol that captured the essence of the person God created them to be. Such a word or image would be a good one to draw on the center of an altar cloth. You might also approach your altar cloth as our church group approached ours on the pilgrimage to England, adding words or pictures to the edges of a cloth over the days and years as an ongoing testimony to God's speaking and working in your life. Pilgrims who have taken an altar cloth with them on a journey and have written words or drawn symbols of God's presence on it along the way can bring it home to be used in the ordinary space of the personal altar as a reminder to remain a pilgrim at heart.

We can also use a cloth that reminds us of a certain calling in our life. My involvement with Amistad, a mission to the Quechua people of Bolivia, has taken me on many journeys to Aramasi, a little impoverished village high in the Andes. There the women weave with brightly dyed llama wool on wooden sticks. One of the women once asked me what they might weave for visiting North Americans. Given my interest in home altars, I suggested a small two by twelve foot cloth with crosses on each corner. They now make these altar cloths regularly, and my small purchases of them provide a means of support for these destitute women. The cloths are not only beautiful and made-to-order, but they also serve to remind whomever uses them of Christ's call to care for the poor.[4]

Objects. The first object to choose for a personal altar is the central permanent one that designates the space as a place for worship. This may be a cross, perhaps one from a family member or from a retreat that played a significant role in personal faith history. A candle is often helpful, since lighting it can help designate prayer time and space on a regular basis. A first object might be a simple replaceable item or might be chosen for its personal meaning as a gift or because of its form such as a cross, candle, or icon. After choosing these items, it is helpful to include the ones that are regularly used in worship or faith study, such as a Bible, devotional text, or journal. Sometimes, for the sake of space, these can be placed on a shelf or drawer underneath the altar surface or nearby.

The next objects to choose for the personal altar are those that reveal the experience of God in an individual's life in unique ways. When I work with people in creating their own personal altars, I ask them to answer the following question in choosing items for their altar:

What are the times, events, actions, or traditions in your life that are sacred in some way to you? Now think of an object that would symbolize each one.

One man I know put a pencil on his altar, a reminder that he needed to plan his faith journey but also be willing to erase and change plans as necessary. One woman put a teapot on her altar, explaining, "There's nothing that can't be helped by a cup of tea." Another woman chose for her altar a letter opener that she uses to open letters from family and friends that bring encouragement. A love of hiking might lead a person to choose a miniature walking stick for the altar; a gift of music might be represented by a guitar pick. A family heirloom that also has religious significance, such as your grandmother's prayer beads, is another worthy item for the altar.

The personal home altar allows for individual worship, but through the objects on the altar as well as the prayers offered there, it connects us with the much wider communion of saints. Items of personal meaning from family members or friends serve to remind us of the community of care that constantly surrounds us. When we worship in the presence of these objects, we are connected not only to the God of all but also to the people who are our companions on our faith journeys. My worship is deepened by items on my altar that allow me to sense the love of my fellow travelers in faith: the candle from my sister, a pewter angel from a dear friend in New York, a woven bracelet with my name on it, a gift from friends far away in Bolivia.

Praying on behalf of others at our personal altars is another way of tapping into the larger community of believers. As Christians, we are called to offer intercessions for the many people in our community and around the world who are in need. By incorporating objects on our personal altars that represent the intentions of others, we can remind ourselves to pray for them. I have a Communion chalice on my personal altar, and in it I put slips of paper on which I have written the names of those I want to remember in intercession. This helps my poor memory and my tendency over time to forget to pray for those to whom I have said, "I'll keep you in my prayers." My chalice of names is not only a reminder for me but also an offering to God. A friend of mine writes the names of people for whom she prays on slips of paper and places them under a wooden cross that lies on her altar. Another friend makes her intercessions as she lights the candle on her altar each morning. She has particular people she is committed to remembering before God at any given season. A journal can also be used for this purpose; a woman I know uses a journal to record prayers offered as well as answered. As a place of intercession, the personal altar allows us to come into the community of believers and to draw friends and family, people in need, and even our enemies to God.

Another way of offering prayers at a home altar is to create an artistic rendition of the Western Wall in Jerusalem. I first saw this in the little prayer room at Bon Secours Retreat Center outside Baltimore, Maryland. An artist had woven together cloth tubes in a rectangular braid that hung on the wall above the little altar. Retreatants could write their prayers on a little piece of paper, roll the paper, and stick it in a crevice of the wall, similar to those who pray at the Western (Wailing) Wall. I have made my own little wailing wall by weaving ribbon on a latch hook canvas and leaving loops where pieces of paper can be put. Framed, the canvas can hang above the altar as an ongoing place for prayers.

Some objects on a personal altar will remain constant, such as the family Bible, a special candle, or a cross from your grandmother. Other objects may be added or rotated as God's presence appears in particular ways over the days and years. In this way, the personal altar evolves as your relationship with God grows. Like a secret box of love items shared by a couple, the personal altar can be the place where we recognize and give thanks for our love relationship with God. Just looking at it reminds our hearts of the love expressed, the secrets shared, the faithfulness lived out.

Special Uses for Personal Altars

The personal altar can be rearranged or set up anew for a celebration or special day of remembrance. Using a personal altar in new ways helps keep it alive as a place of worship. As a rallying place for new celebrations as well as an anchoring place for daily prayer, the personal home altar gives physical expression to our heart's cry to worship God through all of life.

Seasons of the church year can be remembered at home through the personal altar. For example, during Advent, a small Advent wreath might replace the normal candle. During Lent, symbols of things given up, whether chocolate or wine or angry words, or symbols of service taken on, such as praying for neighbors or bringing flowers to the sick, can be placed on the altar. A devotional guide for the season can have a place on the altar as well. At Easter, you might cover your altar with bells, flowers, or with personal signs of resurrection in your own life. During personal seasons of life, such as beginning adulthood, midlife, or retirement, the altar can be used for special faith reflection. For example, during young adulthood, symbols of one's own sense of identity and vocation might be added: a set of scales for a call to pursue justice, a stone for a geologist, or a paper heart for a call to compassionate service. During retirement, items for joyful play or for lifelong service might be central such as a fishing lure, a songbook, or a hammer.

Personal altars can also be designed around themes. For example, Judy King, a sculptor in Austin, Texas, who teaches workshops on home altars, developed one altar with the theme of "Everyday saints—women among us." The altar cloth was crocheted by her grandmother, and items on the altar represented various other women of faith who had influenced her. She used the altar as a workshop centerpiece, and its presence invited the women present to consider the women of faith who had helped form them.

Although the personal altar can be used for a variety of special purposes, I always return to it as a treasured place for my own personal worship, which I experience much as I experience worship in the larger church. After a busy week of work activities— seeing clients, giving workshops, returning phone calls—I arrive at church on Sunday with a sense of comfort and expectancy. Because I have been there so many times before, I easily enter the flow of worship songs and settle into the nourishment provided by Scripture readings and hugs of peace from fellow believers. It is a place where I can refuel and offer myself in gratitude to God each week. That same sense of returning for refreshment as well as spiritual nurturing greets me when I sit before my personal home altar, a miniature throne of God that is adorned so personally with my lavish little reminders of God.

Family Altars

The four-year-old son of a friend of mine called out to his father one day to come and look at something he had made. He had carefully laid out a cloth, a candle, a cup, and crackers on the piano bench and said with delight, "It's feast time!" My friend realized that his young son had prepared a feast for his family as he had seen it done in church and had learned in his Good Shepherd catechesis work there.[5] They shared spiritual Communion together in their home that day in a way neither of them will ever forget.

Jesus said that when two or three are gathered together in His name, He is right there in the midst of them. Our gatherings with other Christian believers are not as often in the church as in the everyday situations of family life: in the bustling kitchen, in the car with children belted in place, or even in the bathroom sharing a sink and mirror. I have seen Jesus in the smiling, mashed-potato-splattered face of my toddler and in the wrestling match on the living room floor between my husband and our three sons. I have heard Jesus in my teenager telling me and my older son to stop yelling and start forgiving during a fight one afternoon. My four-year-old has offered me Communion while he solemnly distributed pieces of bread during dinner, carefully giving one to each member of the family, as he must have seen it done in church so many times. While a personal altar in the home is a place for individual devotion, the family altar is for use by all the members of a family who live together on a regular basis. The family altar seeks to capture the essence of the encounters of love and forgiveness that are part of a family's journey with God.

Worship within the family has a strong foundation in all Christian traditions. In the Orthodox Church, the hymns sung at a wedding as the bride and groom are led around the altar are the same hymns sung at the ordination of a priest as he is led around the altar. Orthodox parents, who are charged with bringing their children up in the faith, are considered to be the priests in the family for the purpose of bringing them up in the faith. The Roman Catholic Church in recent years has developed a renewed emphasis on the home, to the point of calling it the "domestic church." This church offers tremendous training and resources to family-life ministers and parents who wish to develop their faith within the family.[6]

Protestants draw strongly on the Bible, which gives parents a crucial faith role in bringing their children up "in the training and instruction of the Lord" (Ephesians 6:4). The actual practice of family worship within Protestant communities in many places is referred to as the "family altar."[7] Evangelical Christians in the last few decades have also sought to take more initiative in the faith education of children at home, as evidenced particularly by the development of the home-schooling movement.

Worship in the home is a Christian tradition, but as more and more time is spent outside the home, in extracurricular activities or general rushing about, it can be difficult for modern families to establish worship as a regular practice. When families do spend time at home, television and other leisure activities serve as ready distractions. Too often, Christians leave the faith instruction of their children to the church, even though most faith traditions consider parents to be the primary teachers of the faith. (Sunday school originated for the instruction of orphans, who had no parents to train them.) Amidst all these challenges and distractions, the family altar can be a wonderful tool for Christians of all traditions who wish to restore faith training and worship in the home.

While I have a personal altar in my bedroom that I use for my private devotions, there is a family altar in our living room for family worship. Because of limited space, we have placed our little family altar on top of a wooden stereo speaker that sits beside our sofa. The altar is not elaborate or central in the room, but it must have a quiet draw, because it does evoke comments from visitors. Our family altar is draped with a simple cloth on which our children have drawn pictures of a factory and a frog. My husband came up with the idea of using a factory to symbolize our family, since our hope is that people enter into the family, experience work on their character and emerge useful to the kingdom.

The frog, a creature of transformation, represents the transformation we hope to experience in Christ. The objects on the altar include a cross made of Popsicle sticks, a tennis ball, a wooden duck, a dried red leaf, and an old watch. It might look like an odd collection, but each item has a story that reminds us of God's presence in our lives. The cross of Popsicle sticks was a gift from orphaned children in Bolivia given at the conclusion of a retreat that my sons and I offered there. It is a symbol to us of Christ's love, which comes back to us whenever we give it away. The tennis ball and the duck represent the ways in which we spend time together to strengthen family health and relationships: playing tennis and, for the guys, duck hunting. The red maple leaf reminds us of our extended family in Virginia and the family farm there, where our souls are renewed in nature.

While a personal altar serves as a place to honor one person's relationship with God, the family altar provides a common gathering place for faith focus within the home. It is a communal altar space, designed and used by the family as a whole in their dedication to and worship of God.

Purposes of Family Altars

The very act of creating a family altar with many members participating can serve to highlight God's centrality and presence within family life. Much like personal altars, the ongoing display of a family altar within a home provides a visible sign of faith for both family members and visitors.

Although creating a family altar as a one-time activity can be valuable experience in itself, the greatest value of the family altar comes from using it regularly for family prayer and devotions. Roman Catholic, Orthodox, and Protestant traditions all regard the family altar as the place where families gather for regular Scripture reading, prayer, and devotion. In a sermon entitled "Restoring the Family Altar," one Presbyterian minister said, "It appears that God's people have long forgotten that the spiritual strength of their church is directly proportional to the spiritual strength of the families which make up their church. And Christian families who are going to be a spiritual blessing and benefit to the church are those who, as a family, worship the Lord at home."[8] Kelly Haack, a Christian author and workshop facilitator writes in an article for the Lutheran family ministries resource, "While some homes may have a physical altar built of wood or other materials, the family altar is . . . more than physical space. . . . It is the picture of a family as they come together before God."[9]

Though the specific traditions may vary, the value of family worship does not. Family researchers have discovered that there is truth to the saying that the family who prays together stays together.[10] Family worship times that involve praying, reading Scripture, and teaching strengthen family bonds and the family's experience of faith. Even if a simple rote prayer is all that can be managed, the routine of daily prayer still sinks in. Whether saying the rosary, memorizing Bible verses, or singing hymns, the family that prays together invites faith to take root in their lives.

The family altar provides a regular place where the family can gather for whatever simple or elaborate worship they choose to use as a family. The symbols there of God's presence in their particular lives makes this an altar that represents the specific faithfulness of God of their own family life and invites their ongoing growth in faith as a family together.

Creating a Family Altar

The main distinction between what I call a personal altar and a family altar in this book is that the family altar is created by all the family members together and is used primarily for family devotions and worship. While the varieties of choice of place, cloth, and objects are similar to those of the personal altar, each of these choices is usually a group decision. The altar's presence reminds a family of their centeredness in God, and its use becomes a part of developing faith rituals.

Place. When choosing a place, families must first decide if they want the altar to be in a communal living space or somewhere more private. This decision might be based on how the family plans to use the altar and how often. If your family is most often together at meal times, placing the altar in the kitchen or on the dining room table might be appropriate. Many families chose to place a small table in their main living or family room for their family altar, or, if your family prefers to pray quietly as a family or individually, a secluded place such as a corner of a quiet room might better accommodate your needs.

Some families I know have come up with creative locations for their altars. These include:

—The living room mantelpiece, decorated with two hanging candles and two huge icons

—The upstairs hallway, a central yet private spot

—A downstairs powder room, which has been turned into a private prayer closet

Another family has its altar on the second-floor landing of their home. The mother describes what often happens when her daughters bring a new friend to the house. The friend will pass right by lovely and interesting things on the desk or the bookcase nearby, but when she gets to the family altar she will usually notice it, pause, and ask about it. "That's our family altar," one of her daughters will say, and off they will go. It is a familiar, comforting part of the home to her daughter, with a mysterious draw for young visitors.

Cloth. Many families choose a favorite old family cloth, a cloth that represents the family's heritage, or a cloth that represents the family's stage in life, such as a baby blanket, but a fun family option is to create your own family altar cloth. In one class I taught, I brought rectangles of plain white cloth and cloth markers for families to create their own altar cloths. I sent them home with the assignment to imagine their family's faith and call to God and then draw a picture to represent that. The next week the classroom wall was lined with cloths as colorful and different from one another as I could imagine, each with one or several children standing by, eager to explain their masterpiece. The various images included an enormous, multicolored rainbow as the family's symbol of hope, an impressionist garden with family members depicted as different fruits, and a vine weaving around the edges of the cloth with a leaf at each corner that contained a word representing the gifts of one member of the family.

You can also employ your family's talents in creating a family altar cloth. If there is a quilter in the family, he or she could piece together squares of cloth from each member of the family. The squares could be taken from a favorite garment, chosen to show each person's favorite color, or designed by each person. A creative sewer in the family could sew a cloth based on the input of the whole family.

Objects. The items on the family altar are chosen to indicate the working of God within the extended family, both in generations past and in the family today. The questions I like to ask families who are preparing an altar are slightly different from the questions I ask people who are creating personal altars:

*What are the times, events, or traditions in your family life
in which you experience God's presence?
What objects might represent them?*

You can choose objects for your family altar that represent ways in
which God has worked among the family as a whole, or you can
invite each member to choose one individual item for the altar
that represents them.

Additional questions to help in choosing objects for a family
altar include:

*What are special family traditions or specific instances of
God's working in your family's life?*

A little Christmas angel on one family's altar calls to mind a
Christmas years ago when the children heard a loud noise
upstairs and asked their mother what it was. In a spur-of-the-
moment attempt to conceal her husband's secret Christmas activities
in the attic, the mother said, "It's the Christmas angel." That
Christmas the parents left a present under the tree signed "the
Christmas angel," and every year since then another present is left.

What activities contribute to the growth of family relationships?
One woman has a Land O'Lakes butter container on her altar, a sign
of how she and her father were drawn together through cooking.
("Any good recipe starts with a stick of butter," she explained.)

In what ways do you encourage loving communication within the family?

A cassette tape has a central place on the altar of a couple who kept in touch with their daughter while she was in Africa with the Peace Corps through her tapes home.

How do you stay connected spiritually?

One family includes a set of ceramic hands on their altar to represent their holding hands in prayer around the table before each meal.

What are some examples of God's grace to the family in times of conflict or pain?

The altar used by one couple holds a set of wedding ducks from South Korea that they use to illustrate how the relationship is going. They set the ducks facing each other when things are going well and turn them away from each other when they are upset and in need of reconciliation.

What are your family's particular calls to service?

This may be the daily call of family life, perhaps represented by a baby bottle, or a certain service taken on, such as a commitment to drive for Meals on Wheels, which could be symbolized by car keys on the altar.

The family altar usually begins as a group project in which all the members consider the connections to God and to one another that are crucial to the family. Over time, different members may add items or replace old ones. The altar can evolve as children grow, as ways of connecting change, and as traditions develop. From time to time the whole family might decide to overhaul the family altar. Whatever its form, the family altar remains a place for worship and for remembering God's works. Like the seemingly unrelated items of a collage that have been pasted together to create beautiful art, so the items configured on a family altar produce spiritual art that is an offering to God of thanks and prayer.

Uses of Family Altars

A wonderful time to begin a family altar is at the beginning of a family, during an engagement. One couple described to me how they took time in their premarital work to plan a family altar. They considered the values and traditions of each of their families of origin and deliberated about which of these they would want to bring into their marriage. Then they discussed the spiritual practices that would help them keep certain values and traditions and build a strong faith base. Objects representing both old and new values were combined to make their own family altar. In planning their altar as they prepared to embark on married life together, they established a tradition that would have particular significance for their relationship. On an anniversary, a couple might wish to create an altar of thanks with items that represent the gifts of their marriage, the graces they have been given in tough times, and the hopes they have for the future.

If a family grows to include children, making a family altar is a great way to involve them in developing a sense of God at home. Asking children to contribute to the altar their own symbols of God's presence gives everyone in the family a fresh perspective on faith. When my youngest son was very small, he loved the miniature train that circled the Houston zoo and was especially fond of the moment when it entered a tunnel. At every meal, he insisted on including thanks for the "choo-choo train going through the tunnel!"—a train was sacred to his sense of gratitude to God. We suggested he put a toy train on our altar. Another time, we were discussing things for which we were grateful. One son said he was grateful that he was not a giraffe. When asked to explain, he said he had seen a television program that showed baby giraffes having to drop six feet to the ground when they were born, which made him glad to be a human. So he put a toy giraffe on the altar that was a sign to all of us of his gratefulness to God that day.

The family altar is particularly helpful in engaging young children in worship, because the physical setup of the altar and the objects on it give them tangible ways to envision and express faith. By assigning children roles in home worship, their sense of themselves as real members of the body of Christ is further developed. Carol Nyberg, an instructor for the Catechesis of the Good Shepherd, a program that applies the principles of educator Maria Montessori to the spiritual formation of young children, gives children a key role in worship. In her classroom, a shelf holds a number of possible objects for the prayer table: candles, crosses, flowers, figures of biblical characters, and prayer cards (with just one or two words on them, such as *Alleluia, Jesus, Emmanuel,* or *Hail Mary*). The youngest children are given the role of prayer leader, which means they get to choose the objects from the shelf to place on the little prayer table for the day's worship. She has found that this transforms the worship, with the children thinking of it as their own practice rather than the teacher's. This approach can be taken with the family altar as well by having children set the home altar for the day or lead songs or prayers.

The family altar also helps in celebrating the church year with children. For Advent, a time of waiting and preparing, symbols of opportunities to wait on God and others during the weeks leading up to Christmas can be added daily; these might include a receipt from a store with particularly long lines, a post office notice of a package to be picked up, and a bulb of a flower that grows slowly. At Christmas, one family gradually assembles the Nativity scene by adding new items every day, telling stories as they go and building up to the Christ child arriving on Christmas Day. If you place a Nativity scene on your family altar, pieces of straw can be added to the manger for each kindness offered by one family member to another over the weeks leading to Christmas. During Lent, one family makes the altar much barer and places on it a vase filled with branches and sand instead of flowers and water. At Easter, another family fills the altar with bells that they can ring throughout the season as they sing hallelujahs and proclaim that Christ has risen. Making creative and whimsical objects for the altar, such as balloons tied to the altar for Ascension Day and paper doves to represent the Holy Spirit on Pentecost, is a way to celebrate the season while involving the whole family. A friend from Ireland remembers her family creating a May altar in honor of Mary and a June altar in honor of the Sacred Heart of Jesus. The family altar can be used to celebrate various saints' days and feast days in whatever creative way a family wishes. In this way, the altar becomes a living opportunity for faith remembrance and for celebration particular to each community, each family, and each individual.

Aside from their use in special celebrations in the church year, family altars can help celebrate almost any event and can be used to develop special faith activities through the year. When a member of the family has a birthday, he or she can be allowed to create his or her own altar for the day with special items that represent the previous year or wishes and prayers for the coming year. Activities involving the altar can be incorporated into any family holiday, making it central to the celebration and reminding the family to have an awareness of God even in everyday life. A mother I know makes a family altar at Thanksgiving and asks each grown member of the family to bring something from his or her family life and place it on the altar as a symbol of the year.

In addition to its use by the family for worship together, the family altar can be used by individual family members throughout the day. Some individuals in a family may choose to create a personal altar of their own; others may prefer to use the family altar as a place for their individual devotion. The family altar should be seen as a place for anyone to pray anytime, alone or in any grouping. Kenneth Kremer, editor of *Lutheran Parent*, writes, "As a natural response to God's grace, Christian families also build family altars. . . . The frequent visits family members make to the family altar are consistent with the endless and abundant flow of God's blessings."[11] A friend of mine used the family altar in her home to help in her own and her children's grieving when her husband died. She put a large candle on the altar and told her children that anytime they wanted to remember their father they could light the candle and sit there. The altar became a place where each child could go to be alone in grief without having to say he or she was sad and missing Dad. If it seemed appropriate, my friend would join the child at the altar, starting quiet conversation or sitting in silence in front of the candle.

Extensions of the Family Altar

If you find that the family altar enhances your awareness of God and enriches your family's worship, you may decide to scatter icons, religious pictures, and candles throughout the home in an effort to make the whole home a larger temple for God.[12] Another possibility is to set up different altars in different rooms for various members of the family, for different purposes, or devoted to particular patron saints. Sometimes using a family altar will inspire children to create their own personal altars in their rooms or by their beds. The personal altar might include an icon or an image of a special patron saint or biblical figure that they wish to keep nearby as a reminder of the loving presence and prayer of the larger body of believers. The personal prayer space might be as simple as a picture of a grandparent, aunt, or godparent who prays for them.

Using Family Altars with Groups

During one Advent season, I decided to go against the culture's pull to busy, loud, highly decorated, and well-stocked holiday parties. I invited friends to a "Quiet Advent Gathering" with the request that dress be "simple comfortable" and guests bring only a short Scripture passage, poem, or inspirational reading. I set chairs in a circle around my living room coffee table, on which I arranged my Advent wreath and a circle of plain purple votive candles in glass holders. After everyone arrived, I lit the candles on the Advent wreath on my coffee-table-turned-home-altar and read a few sentences from Scripture and from Christian writers[13] about the rare, precious gift of shared silence and waiting. We then sat together for twenty minutes of silence, and out of that silence people slowly read their offerings, often allowing for quiet space in between readings. At the conclusion of the gathering, I invited everyone to take a small votive candleholder and write with a glass marker the word or phrase from the readings that had spoken most deeply to them. They were given these to take home and light in their own quiet prayer times during the rest of the Advent season. I have had more people thank me for that untraditional holiday gathering than I ever have for a fancy dinner party.

One family creates a family altar in a special way with extended family members who are gathered at their home for

Christmas. Before dinner everyone is asked to take time in a guest room where a table has been set up with construction paper, scissors, magazines, wrapping paper, and ribbon. There they are to make a symbol with the art supplies of a gift God has given them that year that money can't buy. When they finish their creation, they wrap it up and place it in the middle of the dining room table. During Christmas Eve dinner, the family takes turns opening the presents and trying to guess what each item is and who put it there. Eventually each person tells his or her story, and in the process the true gifts of God are celebrated around this family altar.

Ideas for Workshop Leaders

In any regular class for families, a helpful devotional start can be for a family to present its own family altar. Another possibility is to use one session, preferably at or near the beginning, for everyone to present his or her family altar. As members share, everyone gains a sense of the holiness of family life in all its variety and individuality. The altar provides a way for members of the class to get to know one another as they offer thanks for family life.

Sara Fontana, a famly advocate in the Diocese of Galveston-Houston Family Life Ministries, also uses the family altar as a basis of community building in family retreats called "The

Story of Us." She asks parents in advance to bring to the retreat one item that best symbolizes their own family of origin, recognizing the spiritual heritage of family for several generations. The first evening, each family is asked to put together a family altar. Parents have to show the object they have brought and tell their children the story of their own family as they put it on the altar. The families then construct an altar that represents their current family. After building the altars, each family has one person stay at their table to explain its altar while others circulate to hear the stories from their fellow participant families. Those who stay to tell and those who wander to listen switch at one point so everyone can fully participate. In this retreat, the family altars stay up all weekend as a continuing family and faith conversation piece. During the community Mass, each family places a symbol from its family altar at the foot of the main altar.

Sara also uses the altar in powerful ways in catechetical work. She asks participants preparing for first Communion to place the things for the church altar on one table, and then on another table next to it to place things from the home that are similar. So just as the linens, candles, and Bible are placed on the church altar, a place setting is on the home table, perhaps with a Bible or devotional book that is read at the start or end of a family meal. The two places are connected as places for gathering and worship, the church and the home church. In another session, participants are invited to each draw something representative of themselves on a square of cloth. All of the squares from the class are sewn together and made into a center section of an altar cloth to be used at their first Communion, and afterwards it is unsewn and sent home with each participant.

For confirmation, participants can each construct an altar that represents spiritual milestones in their life or personal ways in which they experience a relationship with God. They could also draw these on an altar cloth that could be used for their own small altar at home to encourage their developing faith journey.

When I train lay chaplains with the Community of Hope, I present the family altar as a group exercise. Each member of the Community of Hope is encouraged to create his or her own family altar and to affirm God's working in the lives of their family members over time. Then each person brings to the larger group one item from their own family altar to place on a common group altar that represents a new-formed family in Christ. The physical representations and the story-telling of such personal items move participants in any group palpably to a new level of community.

I encourage these lay chaplains to offer the family altar as a way of bringing comfort to hospitalized patients or anyone who has to be away from their home environment in a difficult time. They can turn the windowsill, ledge along the wall, or dresser into their own little personal altar. They may choose pictures of family members, familiar items from home, objects that recall fun and funny times to give lightness, or symbols of God's presence with them. Favorite music can add sound to the atmosphere, and gifts of flowers added to the altar. Just as Gordon McDonald turned a hotel ballroom into a sanctuary, so a hospital room can become a petite personal chapel with reminders all around of a praying, caring community. So an exported family altar is a comforting pilgrim altar during a journey through illness or trial.

One beauty of pilgrim, personal, and home altars is the possibility and creativity that can be expressed through making and using them. My expectation is that readers of this book will take the foundational principles of altar making and create incredible new varieties and uses of altars as the Holy Spirit guides their own unique journeys of faith. These new altars may be individually or in groups, in hospitals, prisons, retreat centers, or homes. Wherever they are built, my prayer is that they will become living means for the worship of God. Altars come most alive as they become used in the practice of spiritual disciplines for growing in relationship with God.

spiritual disciplines for altar life

When I was in grade school, I would make elaborate preparations for Valentine's Day. I would go up to the attic to get the biggest, sturdiest shoe box I could find. After carefully covering the box with pink construction paper, I would spend hours decorating it with red tissue-paper hearts, doily designs, and Cupid arrows. All of this was done to create an appropriate container for the real treasures: the valentines or love notes from school friends that I would collect.

Our altar is like a valentine box for our love relationship with God, a carefully covered container that holds symbols of the most magnificent love relationship of all. Like the valentine box, the altar is lovely in itself but holds true value only as the love relationship remains alive.

Though small in appearance, the home altar can be a tremendous tool to help cultivate faith relationships. The next three chapters will focus on three core spiritual disciplines—the lectio divina, *the* examen *of consciousness, and the practice of remembrance—and the attitudes they develop in us, which are crucial to making the home altar a place of living faith. The* lectio divina *and the expanded* lectio *of life discussed in Chapter 4 develop attentiveness, the attitude needed for seeing and understanding the love initiatives of God. The* examen *of consciousness, explored in Chapter 5, builds a response of gratitude for gifts as well as a contrition and intercession for shortcomings. Finally, the practice of remembrance, as we will see in Chapter 6, encourages faithfulness in our relationship with God over years and generations.*

As we use these disciplines at our home altar it becomes the centering place for the expression of the living love between God and us.

CHAPTER FOUR

Lectio Divina:
Pay Attention

A gift wrapped up I receive: today.
I open one layer at a time.
I smile, try on, admire, enjoy
each moment as the day unfolds.
—*Today's Gift*

The essential starting place of a love relationship, no less with God than with humans, is learning to listen and attend to the other. In our relationship with God, we are called to open the ears and the eyes of our hearts, to fully hear and perceive God's calling and working in our lives. The practice of developing hearts that are open to God is grounded in both biblical and Christian tradition. In the Bible, Jesus often asks those who love Him to stay awake and alert, whether they are walking along a road, waiting with Him in the Garden of Gethsemane, or awaiting His return. Many times He ends a teaching by saying "He who has ears, let him hear" (see Matthew 11:15). St. Benedict teaches that the core of the spiritual life is developing the eyes of the heart. St. Benedict focuses on the critical importance of learning to pay attention to the heart, rather than to external appearances. He asserts that a core piece of spiritual growth involves developing the eyes of the heart. The importance for the spiritual life of having a heart that is open to God's loving presence is undeniable. So how do we attain this attitude of openness and attentiveness to God in our life and in our way of worship in the world?

One of the best traditional ways to develop hearts alert to the personal presence of God is the ancient spiritual practice of *lectio divina*. *Lectio divina*, Latin for holy reading, was the form of careful listening to the reading of Scripture begun in the early church when books were rare. This tradition was kept alive through the Middle Ages and into the present, primarily by Benedictine monks, but was also practiced by Martin Luther and John Wesley. In lectio divina we approach Scripture with a contemplative, listening heart as the living Word of God meant to nourish the soul. Rather than reading long passages and trying to grasp and analyze concepts, we approach a smaller piece of Scripture as if it was a love letter from the Beloved. Whatever passage is chosen is read slowly with an ear toward the particular word or phrase that strikes us personally that day. Once that word is received we meditate on it, allowing it to interact with our own images, hopes, fears, and life movement. Like ear training in music, this practice trains the spiritual ears of the heart to listen for God's particular personal word in every moment. Beginning our day at the home altar with lectio divina can establish an attitude of listening to carry us through the rest of the day.

The home altar as a place for spiritual devotion is naturally a place where we read the Word of God. It appears that Joshua actually wrote the words of the Lord on the stones set up for the altar first built in the Promised Land. With a home altar, as we practice lectio divina, the words that speak to our hearts can be written down and placed on our altar. One way to do this is to write key words on index cards that can simply be laid on the altar. Another way is to use a small spiral notebook to record words that speak to the heart during lectio divina. In this way, I keep a record of words over a period of time or from a whole book of the Bible over time. I sometimes keep the book open on the altar to the page on which I have written my most recent word and meditate on it over a day, week, or season. I may also use an altar book to write passages from poems or devotional readings that particularly resonate with my spirit.

Occasionally a word or passage strikes the heart so strongly that it becomes a permanent part of our spiritual call. This happened to me on a silent retreat day one summer. As I read the Scripture, one passage and one phrase spoke poignantly to my heart. It was the story of Jesus' visit to Mary and Martha, in which Martha complains to Jesus that her sister, Mary, has left her to do all the preparatory work for the meal. Jesus' words to her, "One thing is necessary" (Luke 10:42, New American Standard Bible), caused my chaotic heart to still. The words became my mantra for the retreat, and in the art room I wrote, "ONE THING" in calligraphy on art paper. I framed the paper and hung it above my home altar. Simply looking at these words brings back the calm that washed over my soul and the call in my heart to simple prayer that I experienced in that retreat.

Several weeks later, I visited my twin sister, Beth, in California. She was battling metastasized cancer, and as a mother of two small children she felt overwhelmed trying to keep house and health together. One afternoon, we had some time to ourselves and talked about going out for lunch or doing something special. Instead, we sank into silence together, dozing and taking quiet time with God.

After several hours, I sensed our refreshment and asked Beth softly if anything particular had come to her mind. She asked, "Do you remember the story of Mary and Martha and those words—'one thing,' that Jesus spoke?" "Yes, I do remember those," I told her. "They were the exact words given to me several weeks ago on a retreat day, and they now hang above my prayer table!" We experienced a miraculous spiritual affirmation as we realized that God had again given these same words to sisters for consolation in these days. Before her children returned from the park, we sang a song from the Psalms that we had sung in our teen years together: "One thing have I desired of the Lord, that will I seek after . . . that I may dwell in the house of the Lord, all the days, all the days of my life . . . to behold the beauty of the Lord and to inquire in his temple." We sang the words together with new understanding. Now as I look above my altar and see "ONE THING," the whispered call of Christ and the connection to my sister return in a glance.

The profound personal words that come out of the spiritual practice of lectio divina can become a centerpiece on a personal altar. You can write them on a piece of paper and frame them, as I have done, or you can find an item that symbolizes the meaning of the word and its call, such as a pine cone for bearing fruit or a boat for staying in the boat with Jesus, and place it on the altar. Listening for God's particular words and placing them on the altar helps to cultivate the attentiveness that is essential to all of the faith life.

The *Lectio* of Life

The Bible is the sacred text that forms a central part of most Christian devotions at the home altar. But as most of us are not cloistered nuns or monks, we leave our altar and home for much of our everyday life. If we are to keep our attentiveness to God active throughout the day, we have to read God's wider book of life. This expansion of holy reading is what I call the lectio of life, a spiritual reading of all of life. Every flower, leaf, and blade of grass, each breath of wind, every cloud, and patch of blue sky, each morsel of food, and every person made in the image of God is also the word of God speaking the love of our Creator to us. Love letters, messages, whispers from God to us are everywhere. Our task in growing spiritually is not to change our surroundings but to have the eyes and ears of our heart open to the sights and sounds of God's presence among us.

I expressed this practice of lectio of life once in a poem:

PRAYING WITH OPEN EYES
In my garden, laced with flowers blooming,
as buds appear beneath sky pictures;
at the beach with waves crashing,
as water laps and sand invites,
I pray to God, but closer grow,
not by closing eyes
but opening them wide.

The home altar is perfectly suited to developing this larger spiritual reading of life. Visually, the altar reminds us that our everyday home and pilgrim lives are sacred. Practically, it offers a place where we can put small earthly symbols of our love relationship with our holy Beloved. As we use the altar to reflect discoveries we make in our lectio of life, it becomes an interactive center of our ongoing daily relationship with the living God. The home altar becomes the place of regular worship, like the original altars in the tabernacle and temple where morning and evening prayers were offered. We come to our home altar in the morning to give ourselves as offerings, and at the end of the day we return with our discoveries, sending up the incense of our thanks, praise, and intercession.

Cultivating an Attitude of Attentiveness

The essential attitude needed for the practice of lectio divina and lectio of life is that of attentiveness. Learning to develop such attentiveness is critical to the ability to use a home altar. Without the ability to see and hear the signs of God in our daily lives, we will have nothing to offer at our altars. With open "heart eyes", we will return to our altars with abundant evidence of God's presence along our journey, keeping our spirits and our altars alive. Learning how and where to make these discoveries that fill our hearts and our altars for God is the first step in adopting the practice of lectio of life. Learning how and where to make these discoveries that will fill our hearts and our altars for God is the first step in adopting the practice of lectio of life.

The How of Attending: Stop, Look, and Listen

The saying used to teach children how to cross the street safely is great guidance for how to adopt the basic spiritual attitude of attending at the heart of lectio of life: Stop, look, and listen. Just as children are instructed to stop before crossing the street in order to look and listen for traffic, we need to stop in our busyness to look and listen for God. This stop might be on a busy sidewalk to help a person in need or on a busy day to take a phone call from a frazzled friend or watch a lizard slither across a wall. However, the stopping doesn't always have to be caused by something; we can choose to simply stop what we are doing and spend some quiet time with God. Whether the stopping is for a short amount of time, such as for a daily quiet prayer, or a longer time, such as for a retreat, we are training ourselves to be attentive to God in the midst of everyday life. Stopping, physically or mentally, is the first step in attending to what is coming down the road.

To catch sight of God and hear the still, small voice, we need a different pace, a pace of peace. From time to time, we can take our spiritual pulse to see if we are living heart-healthy, spiritual lives—those low in anxiety and full of peace. I often am so busy, with a calendar so full, that if I get a call from a friend in need or pass a person who needs help, I feel like I don't have time to stop. When I find I have no white space on my calendar or room in my day to respond when God calls in the moment, I try to rein in my activities, slow my pace, and consciously adopt an attitude of openness to God's calls of love, which are so rarely scheduled on any calendar.

Beyond the physical acts of stopping or slowing down is the mental act of being fully present in every moment, another aspect of the attitude of attending. Thich Nhat Hanh, a Buddhist monk and teacher, has written one of the best books about being spiritually present wherever you are, *The Miracle of Mindfulness*.[2] Too often we are so upset about the past or so worried about the future that we miss the present moment. Hanh suggests practicing mindfulness, taking a few hours to be present to each action—pouring water over a tea bag, taking a first sip, petting the dog, lifting the phone receiver and hearing a voice, listening to a child calling. In each moment, we consciously focus single-mindedly on whatever is happening and on being fully present to it.

Another way to practice mindfulness is with walking meditation, in which we focus our attention on our breathing while walking, with each step, trying to stay present in the moment. I remember the first time I tried this. It seemed to me the fullest fifteen minutes of my life. The practice of mindfulness is not easy, and it requires going against some instincts that our culture has instilled in us. Like learning to walk with good posture, learning to be mindful takes practice, persistent and regular practice.

One way of incorporating mindfulness practice into our weekly lives is to use every Sabbath for more deliberate concentration on God. The Sabbath is a time set aside for our rest, for slowing down and attending to God rather than business or busyness. The Orthodox Jews stop every form of work, including flipping light switches and writing with a pencil. We might at least set aside some aspects of our work in honor of the attitude of Sabbath, whether that is answering e-mails, cleaning house, or doing errands. And we can purposely pay closer attention to God throughout the day, both in active worship and slower walking. Tilden Edwards in his book *Sabbath Time* describes the history of the Sabbath within Christian community and offers suggestions for Sabbath rituals that help cultivate this attitude of attention.[3]

Once we stop or slow down, the challenge is to really look and listen deeply wherever we happen to be. One spring day while my aunt and I were on our knees digging in the dirt planting flowers in my garden, she told me memorable words she had heard often from my grandmother, "See what you look at!" My grandmother must have understood the importance of looking closely in the lectio of life.

How often I go someplace or even live someplace for many years and never really notice, never really see, what I am looking at. When I was growing up, there was a big tulip poplar in my backyard. Yet it was forty years later before I really saw a tulip poplar in the way my grandmother advised. I wrote about the experience:

SING GLORY
On retreat, I marvel at
a tulip tree's great height—
limbs laden with tall blossoms
like a candelabra's lights.

Peering close, I notice petals
arranged by artist hands—
like sugar cookies, cherry-filled,
at top one lemon center stands.

Seven ivory tendrils climb
from each cluster's rising story,
each one tipped with amber gold,
as if to sing out glory.

No wonder when I come upon
this tree in listening stillness,
I seem to hear a voice that calls
for me to join the chorus.

When we look deeply, with the eyes of our heart, we see beyond the physical and into the spiritual and find the invisible hand of God in everything. In the same way, listening deeply opens the ears of our heart to God's calls, whether loudly beckoning or silent. When I take quiet time in my bedroom, I often hear the whistle of a distant train or the bells from a nearby church ringing. The train reminds me of God's regular passing, which I frequently do not hear. The bells may be ringing a favorite hymn whose words are just what my heart needs to be joyous in that instance.

Once we have stopped, looked, and listened, we can take what we receive, the fruit of our lectio of life, and place it on our altar as a reminder of God's presence and actions in the world. Like sacraments, which are outward and visible signs of inward and spiritual grace, all of our altar objects are signs of God's hidden working in our everyday lives of faith. In the Nicene Creed, which many Christians profess during worship services, we affirm that we believe in "all that is, seen and unseen." The tokens on our altars remind us not only of the hidden acts that they represent but they remind us also to look always with the eyes of the heart, seeing the spiritual essence beyond the physical object.

A prayer that I might develop these eyes came to me one morning as I looked out my window:

UNSEEN DANCING
The sun comes up and shines bright rays
through unseen air and windowpane,
illuminating fingerprints upon the glass
and dust dots floating leisurely in air.

What unseen life might I see
if I had Spirit light to shine upon my days:
angels steering cars as drivers drift,
simple smiles speaking hope to despairing hearts,
a plateful of peace carried by gentle hands into a room.

If I believe in fingerprints and dust dots
even when the sun's not shining,
help me believe in Spirit works
though eyes see not their dancing.

Once we develop the eyes of the heart, we can see all of Creation in the smallest part of it. The mystic Julian of Norwich saw in a single hazelnut the whole astounding, creative genius and love of God. She writes, "he showed me a little thing, the quantity of a hazel nut, lying in the palm of my hand, as it seemed. And it was as round as any ball. I looked upon it with the eye of my understanding. . . . In this little thing I saw three properties. The first is that God made it. The second that he loves it. And the third, that God keeps it. But what is this to me? Truly, the Creator, the Keeper, the Lover."[4]

The attitude of attentiveness that we develop does not end with looking and listening deeply. As spiritual pilgrims, we are beholden to savor, worship, and perhaps even fall on the ground in gratitude when we are present to scenes of beauty or grace. This worship can be as simple as stopping for one minute to gaze gratefully at a budding mushroom on a morning walk in the woods, giving a brief word of thanks for the swirling colors of a kindergartner's picture, or jumping repeatedly for joy when we manage to retrieve the keys that have been locked in the car. We can then bring whatever we see or hear when we stop, look, and listen to our home altar, in the form of a small symbol, and we can offer prayer and thanks anew for the gifts of God that we have been given that day.

Where to Stop, Look, and Listen

Although we might normally attend to God most diligently in a church service or in a sanctuary, the attitude of attending to God which is the heart of lectio of life is likely to be most useful elsewhere. Two places where the biblical stories would suggest we pay closest attention are ordinary places and relationships.

Ordinary Places and Experiences

A home altar is born out of the understanding that God is present with us everywhere, perhaps most particularly in the midst of our ordinary days and ways. As the psalmist declares, God is present "when I sit and when I rise," in "my going out and my lying down," in "the heavens" and "in the depths" (Psalm 139). Learning to see the small and everyday wonders of life is at the heart of a vibrant spiritual relationship with God. Sometimes losses remind us of common blessings. I know a woman who had eye surgery to reverse the gradual loss of eyesight she experienced as a result of diabetes. After the surgery, she commented, "The trees are beautiful, the sky is beautiful, the telephone poles are beautiful." I do not usually thank God for the lovely telephone poles, but she realized that to see anything was a gift. She helped me see with new wondrous eyes everything in front of me. A number of years ago, my cousin had a serious asthma attack that left her laboring for every breath for more than twenty-four hours. Hearing of her experience gave me a renewed gratitude for every breath I take.

A number of saints, holy people, spiritual writers, and poets have explored the idea and the importance of attending to God in the everyday. St. Benedict encourages his followers to see the sacred in the ordinary and to learn to see and serve God through daily work and simple hospitality. St. Ignatius of Loyola encouraged people to find God in all things. Perhaps the best book on attending to God in the midst of ordinary work is *The Practice of the Presence of God*, by Brother Lawrence, a Carmelite lay brother who found he could worship God better when peeling potatoes in the kitchen than in the chapel.[5]

French Jesuit Jean-Pierre de Caussade writes in an exquisite little book entitled *The Sacrament of the Present Moment* about the wonder of being present to God's presence in every moment and happening of every day. Caussade speaks of the sacramental nature of presence, which he likened to the sacraments with which we are more familiar: the Eucharist, baptism, and marriage. He says, "Those who have abandoned themselves to God always lead mysterious lives and receive from him exceptional and miraculous gifts by means of the most ordinary, natural, and chance experiences in which there appears to be nothing unusual. The simplest sermon, the most banal conversations, the least erudite books become a source of knowledge and wisdom to these souls by virtue of God's purpose. This is why they carefully pick up the crumbs which clever minds tread under foot, for to them everything is precious and a source of enrichment."[6]

The German poet Rainer Maria Rilke understood this concept, explaining in *Letters to a Young Poet*, "If your everyday life seems poor, don't blame it; blame yourself; admit to yourself that you are not enough of a poet to call forth its riches; because for the creator there is no poverty and no poor, indifferent place."[7] He notes that even if we were forced to live in a prison cell, we would still have the treasure of our rich memories. To a poet, which is what we spiritual beings are at our core, all can be experienced with wonder. The small crumbs that nourish us, the memories that enlighten us, these are what we bring to our personal altars each day. The personal altar is designed for such use: with no requirements for what should be on the altar or how the items should be arranged, we can feel free to bring to the altar the objects we discover when we pay attention to God, changing it every week, every day, or even every hour.

Out of the wonders of Creation, a particular sight or sound might become a private message of love from the Creator to us. A permanent symbol of that sight or sound might have a central place on our personal altar, like a special love symbol drawn on the top of a valentine box. My own particular sign from God that makes my heart melt is a beautiful sunrise, sunset, or moonrise. Above my personal altar is a permanent picture of a moonrise, the icon of sorts that points me to my Creator God. A young woman once told me, "When it rains, I take that personally. It seems whenever I am down or in need of knowing God's love, it rains, and I am comforted." Her altar picture might be of a rainstorm, representing God's tears for her. The personal altar allows us to celebrate the uniqueness of our love relationship with God with symbols of the signs of our sacred love in everyday life.

Even when God makes extraordinary appearances, it is often in quiet ways or ordinary places. We see this in a number of biblical accounts of God's appearing to the people. The angels who visit Abraham and Sarah come on a hot afternoon and eat a hospitable meal with them in their tent. Moses is tending his father-in-law's flocks in the desert when he sees the burning bush. God speaks to Elijah not in the whirlwind or the earth-quake or the fire but with a still small voice. Joseph is asleep in his bed when God speaks to him in a dream. The angels appear to the shepherds in a dusty country hillside where sheep graze. Simon and Andrew are fishing at the Sea of Galilee when Jesus calls them to follow Him as disciples. Paul is struck down as he walks along the road (Genesis 18:1–16; Exodus 3:1–4ff; 1 Kings 19:11–13; Matthew. 1:20–24; 4:18–20; Acts 9:1–19). Even today people find God's presence amidst the ordinary events of daily life. When I ask retreatants to think of their most palpable experience of God's presence and then ask where it occurred, they say things like the kitchen early one morning, or out on the lake fishing, or one night in the bedroom listening to music, or on a hike in the woods. These examples tell us that it is likely we will see God or hear God's voice somewhere in the course of our everyday activities.

Sometimes the place where God appears is ordinary, but the timing is extraordinary. A young woman who was struggling with her grief over a best friend's death in a car accident told me about one special hike she took in the woods. She explained that for her college graduation her friend had generously given her a bouquet of irises, a favorite flower. Two Sundays after her friend's death, at the exact time they would have been getting together, had her friend been alive, this young woman was walking in the woods and came upon a field of wild irises. A personal gift from heaven was sent at that particular moment of grief to her.

As we encounter God powerfully in everyday places and experiences, whether in miraculous or mundane ways, we can bring signs of those encounters to our altars to help us maintain an attitude of attending. For the young woman who received a gift from God in the woods, a bouquet of irises gracing her altar would bring back that amazement she felt. The personal altar provides an everyday place to return to in thanks for those moments when God has reached down so personally into our everyday lives.

Relationships

Because the heart of the gospel is a call to loving relationship, with God and our neighbor, the experiences of God in the lectio of life frequently have to do with relationships. I once asked a large group of employees of a homeless mission what the best gift in their life had been. As they shared, I realized that almost none of their stories had to do with things. Almost all of them had to do with people: a son who made it home from serving in the army overseas for a mother's birthday, a husband's healing from cancer, a friend's surprise visit.

The call to see God as we encounter others is part of the spiritual seeing that should be represented on our altars. Of course we think first of dear friends and family as those people most sacred to us, and pictures of them deserve a place on our altars. Loving them can be at the same time one of the easiest and one of the hardest things. Mother Teresa, when asked while accepting the Nobel Prize what we might do to further world peace, responded, "Go home and love your family." The challenges and rewards of building and maintaining family relationships are part of our everyday lives and should therefore be reflected on our altars. In addition to our family and friends, however, we are called to love those who might be unknown to us but who need our help and prayers. In his first letter in the Bible, John makes clear that if you cannot love humans, whom you see, you are a hypocrite to say you love God, whom you cannot see. Jesus, speaking of the poor, says, "Whatever you did not do for one of the least of these, you did not do for me" (Matthew 25:45). Therefore, a child we support in a foreign country, an elderly neighbor we look out for, a sick cousin we pray for daily, or a homeless person to whom we take meals, as those representing Jesus in our world, have a place on our altar as well.

In looking for God, whether on a pilgrimage or in ordinary places and people, the only thing we can expect is that God will appear in the unexpected. We may plan to see God at the great cathedral on the last day of a pilgrimage and instead find ourselves being touched by the sun shining in beautiful patterns on weeds growing in the cracks along a trail. We may expect to find God in the music at a concert and instead find God in the person of a new friend made while waiting in line for the over-sold event. All we can do is remember Jesus' admonition to stay awake and alert. And we have help in this: the lectio divina and the lectio of life develop our ability to attend to the loving messages and presence of God in the ordinary places and relationships of our lives.

If attention is the attitude we need to develop to see the gifts of God to us, gratitude is the attitude we need to respond to God. In the next chapter, we turn to the discipline of the *examen* of consciousness to help us develop a response of humble gratitude when we meet God at our personal altars.

CHAPTER FIVE

Examen:
Return Thanks

I have no need of a bull from your stall
or of goats from your pens,
for every animal of the forest is mine,
and the cattle on a thousand hills. . . .
Sacrifice thank offerings to God,
fulfill your vows to the Most High.
—Psalm 50:9-10, 14

The sacrifices of God are a broken spirit;
a broken and contrite heart,
O God, you will not despise.
—Psalm 51:17

"What is the difference between something you get for free
and a gift?" was the question the preacher asked us one Sunday
after Christmas at St. Phillips Episcopal Church in Charleston,

South Carolina. He proceeded to pull out from under the large standing lectern an abandoned umbrella as well as a sweatshirt that he had gotten from the lost and found after they remained unclaimed for many months. Then he brought out a Christmas gift and slowly unwrapped it as he made the point that a gift comes from a giver and becomes special because it represents a person and that person's care for us. The contents turned out to be a cardboard box filled with letters sent from friends and parishioners to him over the last month after his father's death. That gift brought to him an image of multiple faces, words of care, casseroles, and hugs. A gift comes from a giver and calls forth a response of gratitude which binds us together with them in love. The many gifts in our lives are not simply things we got for free. They are gifts from our heavenly parent who desires a relationship with us as receivers of His generous grace. The personal altar provides a meeting place for a living exchange between God, the great gift giver, and ourselves as delighted and grateful children.

In the biblical story of Jesus' healing of the ten lepers (Luke 17:11–19), Jesus highlights the importance of not only offering thanks in the moment but also taking time to return to God with explicit thanks for personal gifts. Ten lepers come to Jesus to beg His mercy. He sends them away and they are miraculously healed. Of the ten, only one comes back to offer praise to God for his healing. Jesus asks, "Were not all ten cleansed? Where are the other nine?"

We too often are like the nine who took their healing and ran or just leaped for joy with their friends. But faith is what makes us well, and we must constantly nurture and grow in our faith by giving thanks to God for all our gifts. A home altar, like a stack of thank-you cards placed in a conspicuous place on our desk, can help us remember to thank God, whether it is for a miraculous healing or a beautiful wildflower found in a meadow.

Historically, people built altars in response to God's appearing and used them in an ongoing way to bring offerings to God. The psalmist writes that the most important offerings to God are thanksgivings and a contrite heart. We can use our home altars in the same way, returning to them daily with offerings of ourselves and our thanksgivings.

An ancient spiritual discipline that teaches us to offer ourselves and our thanks to God on a daily basis is the *examen* of consciousness. Established by St. Ignatius of Loyola as part of his spiritual exercises for faith formation, the examen is a process of reflecting at the end of the day on the day's consolations, or positive movements of the Holy Spirit that bring a feeling of closeness to God, and on the desolations, or times when we feel distant from God. The examen begins by quietly becoming aware of the presence of God and asking for the Holy Spirit's help in reviewing the day. Then comes a mental review of the day, from the perspective of noting times one sensed the most closeness to God and the most distance from God.

For regular use by individuals and families at home, a simplified form of this practice is beautifully described in *Sleeping with Bread*, a book by retreat leaders Dennis Linn, Matthew Linn, and Sheila Fabricant Linn.[1] They suggest we ask ourselves two simple yet profound questions each day:

> "At what moment were you most grateful today?"
> "At what moment were you least grateful today?"

Other versions of these questions include when did you feel most alive and most drained of life or when did you give and receive the most and least love. Another version uses a concrete image that is easy to remember, asking what was your rose, your thorn, and your bud. The bud offers an opportunity to also reflect on something of hope for growth ahead.

This simple form of the examen of consciousness requires us to set aside time at the end of the day for reflection, during which we can detect the movements of the Spirit in us that day. After our experiences of God's gifts during the day, we return home and, like the leper, give ourselves and our thanks to God. The home altar provides a place to return for this time of devotion. If we use our altars to take time before God with these two questions, they will lead us to the offering of both our thanks and our contrition.

Offering Thanks

When we ask ourselves the first examen question, "At what moment were you most grateful today?" we may often find that the moment we settle on is a small one that we did not fully savor at the time: a wave from a child, a creative comment from a co-worker, one bloom bursting from the potted plant outside. Reflection time at our home altars allows us to savor that gift through our memory of it as well as give explicit thanks to God for it. Placing on our altars an item or even a word written on a card that represents the gift makes our thanks more tangible and converts our invisible attitude of gratitude into a visible offering to God. The altar offering can also serve as a reminder to us and to others who might pass by our altar to give thanks again and again for a gift.

The first examen question will many times lead us to recognize not just one gift to be grateful for but the many gifts we have been given through the day. For me, this realization multiplies my thanksgivings in prayer. So I daily send up abundant praise at my humble altar, just as the incense of praise and thanksgiving was offered daily for centuries at the altar in the Old Testament temple.

You might consider setting a little journal on your altar to record the moments for which you are most grateful. Over time, a pattern might emerge that leads to discernment about God's calling in your life, which in turn can guide you in how you devote your time and make decisions. As you align your life more closely with your calling, your thanksgivings will multiply even more.

Asking this first examen question as a family is a way to stay connected with our family members and foster an attitude of gratitude on a corporate level. My husband and I are often running in many different directions, with him frequently traveling away from home. Still, if we can take even a few minutes to share our answers to the examen questions, whether at our family altar in our bedroom or at our "virtual altar" over the phone, we feel as if we are staying in touch at the deeper spiritual level. When we engage in the practice of the examen with our children, whether we are sitting around a family altar or in the "traveling altar" that is the car, these simple questions can make spiritual life down-to-earth and accessible.

Cultivating an Attitude of Gratitude

The practice of the examen and the regular placing of symbols of gratitude on the home altar help to cultivate an underlying attitude of gratitude essential in the spiritual life. A fundamental faith assertion is that God is good, that the creation God made is declared very good, and that all of life itself is a gift.

A first part of this attitude of gratitude is the awareness of all of life as a gift. Thanksgiving has to do with taking nothing for granted, nothing as deserved but rather all as miracle and gift from God. Often in my prayers with my sons at night I will give thanks for the gift of this day of life, remembering the miracle that it was simply to be alive on this particular day. How amazing that all of our body organs kept working for all those minutes and hours. How wonderful all that we could see, hear, feel, taste, and smell. I remember a question to Helen Keller of what she would choose to see and choose to hear if she had two days with sight and hearing. Occasionally I try to imagine today as one of those days in my own life. The practice of the examen and of our prayers at our altar each day must begin with an awareness of the gift and goodness of life.

During my trip to Israel with my son Ben, we visited the Diaspora Museum. Arriving near the end of our last day, we dashed in eager to take in all that we could in a limited time. Unfortunately, the main exhibits were closed due to a bomb threat, and we had to wait in the lobby where we perused a gift counter. A very elderly woman was behind the counter, and I inquired about a piece of jewelry in a shape I did not recognize.

She explained that it was a Chai necklace, made in the shape of the Hebrew letter that stands for life. Ben asked quizzically about what she meant. With her multitude of gorgeous wrinkles from many years of living, she looked straight at us with a twinkle in her eye and said, "I give thanks every day for LIFE." That woman exhibited more of the Jewish spirit of the museum than any of the exhibits we eventually saw. From her core, I took a new gratitude for the miracle of each day of life. A Chai or any personal symbol for that deep essential gratitude would make a good offering on any home altar.

In addition to gratitude for simply being alive, cultivating an attitude of gratitude means learning to see the many small everyday happenings as gifts. As we learn the attitude of attentiveness, we begin to see simple appearances of grace. It is not sufficient just to receive our daily bread or enjoy a beautiful day on the lake or discover a nest of bluebird eggs. Part of living in a faith relationship with God is recognizing each of these as gifts and in turn offering thanks to the Creator.

With a heart of gratitude for the small blessings, the large discoveries and joys become cause for great heart celebration. So the birth of a child, music recital, special anniversary, or winning a good sportsmanship award deserve terrific thanksgiving. The home altar might be turned into a celebratory display of thanks for such occasions.

Probably the hardest step in developing an attitude of gratitude comes in the ability to give thanks in all things, even the difficulties. Giving thanks in hard times comes only from believing somehow mysteriously that God uses all things for good for those who love God. Corrie Ten Boom was able to give thanks for the fleas in the concentration camp, which turned out to be the cause of their not being inspected by the guards so rigorously. I am fortunate if I can give thanks when the toast burns (makes me humble) or my car runs out of gas (I have to learn to ask for and receive help). The second part of the examen will give us even more opportunity for this redemptive aspect of developing gratitude.

Special Seasons of Thanks

In addition to our daily thanks, we can give special thanks during certain seasons of the year. In the Old Testament, God commands the people to bring him their first fruits during harvest time (see Leviticus 27:30; Deuteronomy 12:5-6). This means a tithe of everything, from the land to the flocks and herd. The people choose the best of their harvest and the newborns of their flocks to bring for sacrifice on the Lord's altar. Although neither Jews nor Christians bring animals as offerings today, the principle of offering to God the best fruits of our labor remains as valuable today as ever.

With a home altar, we can honor this principle by simply putting a literal first fruit on the altar. This could be a first tomato from the garden, if we are so fortunate to have one (or a first apple from a tree). One way to apply the principle to our modern life is to bring to the altar the first fruits of whatever we do, be it a first drawing from a toddler, a first report card from a child, a first chapter from a writer, a first deal from a businessperson, or a first trophy from a soccer player. We can offer it simply by laying it on the altar for just a moment and uttering a brief, personal thank you to the Lord, or we can gather with our family in the evening to give particular thanks for this fruit or accomplishment, acknowledging it as a gift from God. On special occasions, we can design a little home service around the altar, perhaps with a few close friends gathered together to offer thanks for whatever first fruit has been harvested.

A more direct way of honoring the harvest time celebration of our ancestors in faith is to build special altar traditions into the celebration of Thanksgiving. The Thanksgiving we celebrate in the United States began in a spirit of gratitude to the Creator, with Native Americans and English settlers gathering to give thanks after their first harvest following a gruesome winter. We continue this celebration today, offering thanks at harvest time even though most Americans no longer personally harvest from the land. Several years ago, I started a new Thanksgiving tradition.

I bought a yellow tablecloth and a pile of permanent cloth markers. When everyone in the family gathered for Thanksgiving, I asked each person to think of what he or she was grateful for that year and to then write a word or phrase or draw a picture on the edge of the tablecloth to symbolize it. Gradually, pictures of musical notes, a big fish, a rainbow, a pet gerbil, and a cap and gown took form in a variety of colors. Each year (when I can find it in the closet), I bring the tablecloth out and have family members add new pictures and words. I imagine it being filled over the years with pictures, along with gravy and cranberry stains, that can bring back memories and stories of thanks. The Thanksgiving tablecloth turns our family table into an altar of sorts for this season.

In the spirit of giving thanks in times of harvest, I have a personal tradition that involves reflecting on the people who have played a part in those moments of the year for which I am most grateful and writing them a special note of thanks. Such notes have gone to a teacher who went out of her way to help one of my children when he was in a tough spot, to a man who stopped to help me when my car died, to a restaurant owner who unexpectedly gave me and a friend a free meal for her birthday, and to a friend who knit me a prayer shawl that wrapped me up in comfort and healing after a surgery. As I write these notes, I offer thanks to God for the harvest of kindness and ask God's blessings on these servants of grace.

Offering Contrition, Thanks for Redemption, and Intercessions

The second question of the examen, which asks us to name the moment when we were least grateful during the day, provides valuable offerings for our altar as well. Our reflection may lead us to offer contrition for failures or sins committed, thanks for God's redeeming of a difficult situation, or intercessions for people who are in pain or in need. Signs of our desolations, which serve to remind us of God's forgiveness and redemption, have an important place on our altars.

When we ask ourselves the second examen question at the end of the day, we may find that we frequently arrive at a regretful behavior or a failure as the moment for which we are least grateful: a lost temper, a missed meeting, a jealous attitude, a temptation taken. Fortunately, the sacrifice God wants most is a contrite heart. With a confession of sin and a request for forgiveness, we gain humility as well as gratitude for grace. An added benefit of this sort of personal reflection is that it makes us focus on the areas of our life that need work as well as prayer. As we bring our desolations to the altar day after day, we may come face to face with a pattern of angry outbursts that destroy relationships, or lateness that conveys a lack of care, or jealousy that eats at our own soul, or inner temptations that are constant struggles. When we find these patterns, we can include symbols on our personal altars that indicate our ongoing struggles: a pot broken because of a lost temper, a card for a missed appointment, a Serenity Prayer card.

Occasionally the moments for which we are least grateful lead to the moments for which we are most grateful and become testimony to God's redemption. A toy recreational van on our family altar represents such an event in our family life. For one family vacation we decided to rent a large recreational vehicle, thinking it would be a fabulous way to see the countryside of Australia. It also turned out to be an incredibly slow way to see the country. On top of that, when the RV broke down in the little mountain town of Braidwood, in the middle of nowhere, we found ourselves packing up all the luggage for our family of five, along with the hamburger, milk and various snacks we had bought, and heading by public bus to the next city, where we rented a small car. We had never been so grateful for a car that went sixty miles an hour. As we drove to our next stop, God treated us to a magnificent sunset, and when we arrived at our destination that evening, we found a motel complete with an outside grill. The RV on our altar stands in our family for the time when God turned a worst-case scenario into a solved problem.

Painful or difficult moments in which God is able to teach us important lessons are also desolations for which we should give thanks. On the last morning of my trip to Assisi, I arose early for a time of prayer. Dressing quietly in the bathroom so as not to wake my roommates, I turned around and suddenly my back was wrenching with pain. I barely made it to the backyard of the convent to watch the day come to light. The pain was so great that I had to lie flat on the firm ground. As I lay looking up at the sky, I pondered what God was trying to say with such an awful injury on the day I was to leave. I imagined hauling my luggage and all the gifts and goodies I had accumulated (why had I bought so many material things?) and started to worry. Then I recalled the words that God had spoken to St. Francis when he was called to poverty and service: "Carry nothing." Unable to carry anything and yet headed home, I learned to be dependent, to ask for help and to be grateful for the community of care. The women I traveled with graciously assisted me, as did Italian strangers all along the way. No longer independent and competent, I reached out in conversation to others whom I might have ignored otherwise. I learned that injury and dependence were gifts, as they created gratitude to God for others. I made it home, hobbling and humbled. I had never before had a back injury and have not had another since. The small words of God to St. Francis, "Carry nothing," written on a card from my pilgrim altar still bring back this life lesson.

When we reflect on the small desolations of our days, we should also remind ourselves to see challenging or painful times as opportunities for God's redemption: the forgotten boots as a chance to go back for another visit with grandparents, the broken vase as a reminder not to get attached to things, the car breakdown as an opportunity to learn to ride the bus and to meet new people, the key locked in the car as a chance for women to work creatively together. Each of us has days full of such small and large difficulties. For believers, these daily desolations allow us to make offerings of contrition, giving thanks for redemption, or receiving communion at God's altar.

Paying attention to the desolations of the day leads us finally to the important offering of intercession for others at our altars. Our desolations often may have to do with a discovery of the pain of a friend or the latest tragedy in the world. A friend's cancer diagnosis, a child's trouble at school, an earthquake in another country—all weigh down our hearts and can be brought to the altar to be lifted up to the throne of grace. In our feeling of helplessness, we cry out to God. In our reflection, we sometimes hear a small way we can respond with aid.

A final gratitude builder on my personal altar is a tiny wooden bowl given to me by a close spiritual friend. It represents the begging bowl used by monks under a vow of poverty who survived only by going out with a begging bowl each day. Their discipline was to be grateful for whatever came into the bowl that day, be it much or little. It reminds me to try to develop that same attitude, being grateful for whatever comes into my bowl each day—in the way of work, gifts, or challenges.

CHAPTER SIX

Remembrance:
Tell the Stories

Only be careful, and watch yourselves closely
so that you do not forget the things your eyes have seen or
let them slip from your heart as long as you live.
Teach them to your children and to their children after them.
Remember the day you stood before the LORD your God at Horeb.
—Deuteronomy 4:9-10

Remember the wonders he has done,
his miracles, and the judgments he pronounced.
—1 Chronicles 16:12

Since my youth, O God, you have taught me,
and to this day I declare your marvelous deeds.
Even when I am old and gray,
do not forsake me, O God,
till I declare your power to the next generation,
your might to all who are to come.
—Psalm 71:17-18

After we cultivate attentiveness to the presence of God in our daily lives through holy reading of life and develop gratitude using the examen to offer thanks to God, we must then remember these stories of God's working. Remembering the presence and works of God keeps our faith, especially through difficult times. But rememberance also ensures that others benefit from our experiences of God and that the next generation will keep the faith.

The home altar serves as the meeting ground for these three spiritual disciplines. We must pay attention to God in order to see what we can bring to our altar. The altar then provides a place for us to give thanks visibly back to God. Finally the altar and items we place there help us to remember the works of God. This final discipline of remembrance is crucial to our developing an essential spiritual attribute for the long term, faithfulness.

Remembrance as a spiritual practice is grounded in biblical tradition, and the Bible itself, as a record of God's creating and relating to the people, serves to help us remember God's working throughout history. Over and over again in Scripture, readers are exhorted to remember the works of God and to tell others, especially those in the next generation, of these works. One of the most poignant examples of this can be found in the story of the first Passover. Before bringing the Israelites out of Egypt, God tells Moses and Aaron to have the Israelites prepare a meal and place the blood of lambs on their door frames, a sign to God to pass over their houses. God says, "Obey these instructions as a lasting ordinance for you and your descendants. When you enter the land that the LORD will give you as he promised, observe this ceremony. And when your children ask you, 'What does this ceremony mean to you?' then tell them, 'It is the Passover sacrifice to the LORD, who passed over the houses of the Israelites in Egypt and spared our homes when he struck down the Egyptians'" (Exodus 12:24–27a).

Today, the Passover seder is a central faith celebration for Jewish families, as it has been for centuries. At every seder celebrated around the world, families remember the miraculous parting of the Red Sea and the deliverance of the Israelites from bondage in Egypt. According to tradition, children ask the questions beginning with "Why is this night different from any other night?", and parents recall the wondrous works of God. The songs that are sung today express the Israelites' delight in the deliverance and their rejoicing afterward.

The foods served remind the family of the story, for example *haroset* (of wine, chopped apples and chopped nuts), for the mortar of brick-making in Egypt, parsley dipped in saltwater for the tears of the Jewish slaves, a lamb for the sacrificial offering, and an egg for rebirth.

At a seder supper, Jesus initiated the central Christian commemoration of the Eucharist. Paul writes of this in his first letter to the Corinthians: "The Lord Jesus, on the night he was betrayed, took bread, and when he had given thanks, he broke it and said, 'This is my body, which is for you; do this in remembrance of me.' In the same way, after supper he took the cup, saying, 'This cup is the new covenant in my blood; do this, whenever you drink it, in remembrance of me'" (1 Corinthians 11:23–25). We can take these words as words to us, making remembrance central to our faith celebrations and our faithful following of God. In order to do this, we must find ways to remember, and one of the simplest and most traditional ways is by using our altars as storehouses for memories.

Altars have always been a common means of remembering the works of God. The Bible describes the early altar Joshua built: "Joshua called together the twelve men he had appointed from the Israelites, one from each tribe, and said to them, 'Go over before the ark of the LORD your God into the middle of the Jordan. Each of you is to take up a stone on his shoulder, according to the number of the tribes of the Israelites, to serve as a sign among you. In the future, when your children ask you, 'What do these stones mean?' tell them that the flow of the Jordan was cut off before the ark of the covenant of the LORD. When it crossed the Jordan, the waters of the Jordan were cut off. These stones are to be a memorial to the people of Israel forever'" (Joshua 4:4–7). The purpose of this altar, a big, permanent gathering of stones, was to be a sign of the work of God to anyone who passed by in generations to come. Seeing it, would cause a person to wonder, to ask about the story, and to worship: which are the same purposes of even our smallest altars and items on them.

All too often in the midst of daily life, we forget the wonders of God. In dry or ordinary seasons, we may question if there is a God or certainly have a hard time remembering God's mighty works. An altar in our home and the items it holds serve the same purpose as Joshua's huge pile of river rocks—to remind us daily of the work of God and the ways in which we have personally witnessed God's presence among us.

Remembrance in Our Day

When my son was thirteen and attending confirmation classes, he asked me and my husband, "How come the Bible stopped being written?" My husband and I looked at each other, both hoping the other would field this question. But as I reflected I realized it was a good question. The Bible records the works of God through history, and God's works continue today. Though the biblical canon is closed, we Christians living today must tell the stories of the continuing works of God. Although we cannot write a chapter of the Bible, our lives and their stories are part of the record of God's working, and they need to be told, recorded, and remembered today as much as ever. The children's Good Shepherd Christian classes make this point to young children when they put out a long, long piece of paper on which the events of history, particularly God's history are written in order: creation, the patriarchs, kings, prophets, and Jesus' ministry.

Placing on our altar visible reminders of God's particular presence in our own or our family's life is a practical way to recall the works of God. When we are building a home altar with a view to remembrance, one question to ask ourselves is "What is the most amazing work of God in my history or my family's history?" We may have only one Red Sea experience— or perhaps none at all—but whatever story stands out needs a symbol on our altar. Mine is a candle given to me by my twin sister, Beth, who was diagnosed with metastasized cancer four years ago and is miraculously alive today. My friend Kathleen might put a shoe on her altar to represent her ability to walk after doctors declared that she would never again be able to. Another friend might place on her altar a picture of her son, whom she was not supposed to be able to conceive.

Often the greatest works of God come in the midst of the most difficult situations. When my sister, Beth, was struggling with her cancer symptoms and treatment, truly her worst of times, she experienced amazing divine miracles, making it also the best of times. The phone call that came just when she was descending into darkness, the mysterious urge to pray that our third sister in Alabama had at the exact hour of a prayer gathering in California, cranes landing on Beth's porch during her prayer time—the examples of God's presence in the middle of her pain go on and on. If her home altar held an object for each of these instances of grace, it would be piled high. She can display signs of just some of these moments to remind her in more difficult hours that God is indeed walking with her.

While any great works of God in our family history certainly need a place on our altar, many of the works that we need to remember are those that may not seem spectacular to an outsider but which we know from experience were a clear divine touch in our lives. Signs of the small evidences of God that are vivid in our minds during spiritually vibrant periods of our life help remind us to keep the faith light burning in dimmer days. A picture of the sun shining brightly would remind me of the times God seemed to be so clearly connecting me with my friend Betsy. A birthday candle is the sign to another friend of an amazing story of God providing exactly forty-eight lawn candles for hope on her darkest birthday. A business card from a restaurant reminds another friend of a surprise free meal on a special day. The little symbols that actually have a story behind them that we can remember with a smile and tell another person, are those that build our faithfulness most clearly.

Whatever the particular works of God in our life, large or small, few or many, the home altar serves as place on which to display items that represent them. Each item on the altar becomes a trigger for a memory of God's goodness. A simple glance at my altar makes my heart recall the amazing works of God and the wideness of God's mercy. And often my heavy heart lifts and I cannot help but smile as I remember.

As we become more attuned to God's presence and the altar is used more over time, it will not be able to hold all the items discovered on a long faith journey. Yet because each item is important and represents a story of God's working, we should not get rid of all the old items when we need to add new items to the altar. A storage container can hold sacred remembrances not in current use. This might be the drawer of the altar table or a cardboard box carefully covered like my childhood valentine box. I have a little trunk into which I put my remembrance items, and I imagine sitting around it with grandchildren, having them pick an item and then telling the family faith story that goes along with it. I can also imagine seasons of dark nights of the soul or hard physical trials in which I might take out these remembrances and spread them out on my bed or on a table to revive my spirits. A family I know keeps a journal on their family altar, and whenever something of spiritual significance happens, they write about it. A journal might also be used to keep a record of items and their stories before the objects are put into storage.

Put together, these altar items or journal pages create a picture of God's faithfulness to an individual or a family through the years. If we use the altar as a way to memorialize the faith works of our lives, it can become a part of an ongoing ethical will. The ethical will, unlike a traditional will, which deals with money and things to be passed on to others, records the traditions and values to be passed on to others. The ethical will may be as simple as a handwritten paragraph or as elaborate as a book, a videotape of family stories, or a collection of stories in a notebook. Although the ethical will is frequently offered after someone dies, it can also be used as a values statement to guide one's living. Making a family altar and completing an ethical will both require the same sort of prayerful, reflective thinking about what is important and how to express it. So the altar can stand as a sort of ethical will on its own or be incorporated into a more extensive ethical will for posterity.[1]

Cultivating the Attitude of Faithfulness

Proclaiming faith for a moment is wonderful. Living faith for a lifetime is monumental. I grasped the enormity of faithfulness sitting at the celebration of my parents fiftieth wedding anniversary on August 11, 2001. My parents are rather unassuming people, not the sort that will find themselves on the front page of the newspaper. Yet as I watched the people gathered to commend them on their keeping of their marriage vows through better and worse, sickness and health, richer and poorer (they like everyone in fifty years had their love tried by poorer, worse, and ill times) for so many decades. I saw two generations of children and cousins not to mention a hoard of friends watching their lives. I was struck by the astounding accomplishment of having lived fifty years of faithful marriage. These quite ordinary people had indeed done something extraordinary that was bearing fruit as an anchor and model for dozens of other marriages which would in turn produce dozens more. The power of faithfulness in a loving relationship is greater than any short-lived extravagance. So too in our relationship with God.

One way to develop faithfulness is to build rituals into our lives. Rituals begun in times of vibrant energetic faith can hold us through dry and difficult seasons. After we were confirmed, my father began praying the bishop's confirmation prayer over me at night. God heard and answered those prayers of my father for my life. That prayer has stayed in my heart and I now pray it over my son at night. My husband prays a prayer at night with our sons as well, always including "help him to grow up to be the man of God you want him to be." One evening when my husband was away, I was praying with my young son who in his time to pray said, "And help Mommy to grow up to be the kind of old woman you want her to be." The youngster who sees their grandmother saying the rosary at the family altar each morning may not join in every day but might find herself pulling out those rosary beads years later in a time or illness or need for faith as a parent herself. Repeated rituals often take hold in some form in the hearts of the next generation.

Faithfulness is built through rituals used over time that become part of our souls. Developing some sort of ritual around the altar helps build core faith patterns for life. That ritual may be simply a two sentence prayer before everyone leaves for the day or lighting a candle with a prayer whenever someone is in need of special prayer. Or it may be a more elaborate weekly time of family prayer with Scripture reading and prayer that includes everyone. The few rituals that are faithfully carried out over many years often are the anchors for faithfulness.

Faithfulness is also built by keeping a love for God nurtured and vibrant. Just as a relationship can grow dull and distant without infusions of care and grace through the years, so too with our faith. When faith expressions seem to be losing any real meaning in individual or family life, finding a way to reinvigorate them keeps them from turning into an ancient dead memorial. So the grace that has been said around the dinner table and remained one set prayer could have a new ending that allows everyone to give a word of thanks. The family altar that becomes dusty might be remade at the beginning of every Advent and Lent or at each family birthday by the birthday person.

Remembering the rituals, remembering to keep love infused with new vibrancy, and finally remembering to tell the stories all build faithfulness. The Bible began with an oral tradition of telling stories that eventually were written down. Our own stories also need telling to keep them fresh for those who witnessed them and to pass them on to those who were not there.

Altars for Storytelling

Just as children ask questions at a seder and the adults tell the story of God's deliverance, so too will visitors in our home ask questions about the items on our family altar, giving us an opportunity to tell our stories. Often a visitor to our home will notice with curiosity a framed watch on our family altar. This leads me to tell them the story of my husband's trip to Russia with a staff member of Prison Fellowship. My husband was visiting a prison outside St. Petersburg for young teen boys and was asked to speak to them one Sunday morning. My husband does not remember much of what he said. He does remember one young boy coming up to him afterwards and thanking him profusely for coming, then pulling a watch out of his pocket.

The boy Alexi handed the watch to my husband in thanks, explaining that it was his father's watch which his father had gotten while serving in Stalin's army. My husband, wide-eyed, turns to the interpreter and says in English, "I can't take that watch. It's probably one of the only things this child owns." The interpreter whispers back firmly in English, "You MUST take the watch. It may be his only opportunity to give a gift." So my husband who has so much more than this child ever will, takes this generous gift from the heart and asks the interpreter to tell Alexi in Russian thanks for this treasured gift. The watch now serves to remind us to be equally generous since we have so many opportunities to give gifts. And whenever someone asks, we tell them of Alexi's widow's mite gift so that they too will be inspired in their giving.

Putting items on your altar that have a story to tell and teach helps the altar to be used for remembrance. Placing the altar in a highly visible place encourages remembering and telling the stories. One mother purposely placed her family's altar in the kitchen, where all the children's friends gather, so that it gives her a ready opportunity to share their faith with visitors. She cautions people not to have such a public family altar unless you are willing to speak, because people will ask questions. She lives out the exhortation of St. Peter (1 Peter 3:15) to be ready to give an account of the hope within us.

Because families often gather for conversation over a meal, having a family altar near the dining table can facilitate its use in faith storytelling. To further encourage faith storytelling, families might want to move the altar to the center of the dining table when gathered for a special meal together. Some families make the dining table the place for their family worship, and so the center of the table could become a natural ongoing altar place, or a candle and a Bible could be moved from a smaller altar space to the table when the family gathers there for prayer.

Through its stories, the family altar becomes the means of transmitting the family faith history, much as the biblical stories were conveyed orally for centuries before being written down. Stories play a central role in the faith tradition of Christians: they make up the Bible, they are what Jesus uses to explain spiritual principles, and they are often what convert us to faith or turn us back to God. Stories are what we remember. The home altar, with its particular set of personal items, evokes curiosity and invites questions, thus providing an opportunity to remember the works of God through stories. In remembering and telling our personal stories of God, we keep our faith alive and pass it on from one person to another and from one generation to the next. When the discipline of remembrance is practiced around our simple altar, it becomes a powerful witness to the working of God in our ordinary, extraordinary lives of faith.

expanded
altar possibilities

Understanding the basic principles for altar making and the core spiritual disciplines for using an altar provides a foundation upon which all varieties of form and use of altars can develop. The great beauty of home altars is that they allow such personal expression and individual creativity for worship of God.

Although I have given some examples of my own and others, use of altars, my hope is for this book is not that it will make any final statement about altars but will instead spawn the new use of altars by individuals and families. I imagine that all sorts of expanded possibilities will develop from the hearts and minds of believers who begin to use altars as a meeting place with God.

In this section, I present two sorts of altar varieties as an additional resource to readers. First I reach out across the world and back through history to briefly describe various ethnic altars in Chapter 7. These alternatives may encourage readers to adopt aspects of their own or another culture's uses of altars in their own homes. Or it may inspire readers to consider how they might develop and expand celebrations of their own making around their home altars. Next I reach beyond the walls of the home to the green garden spaces of nature to suggest possibilities for outdoor altars in Chapter 8. Hopefully these two chapters will leave readers considering their own expansions of altars for worship.

CHAPTER SEVEN

Ethnic Altars: Continue Faith Heritage

Therefore,
since we are surrounded by such a great cloud of witnesses . . .
let us run with perseverance the race marked out for us.
—Hebrews 12:1

At a diversity workshop given by Bea Cunningham, a catechetical leader in Houston, "heritage tables" line the walls. A man from Trinidad has on his table a generations-old picture of some family members, picture albums of current family members, and a figure of the Infant of Prague. He has Caribbean music playing in the background. A Vietnamese nun has covered her table with a red silk cloth on which she has placed baby clothes she wore as an infant, a boat representing her family's coming to America, a statue representing the blood of the martyrs of the Communist regime, and a rosary. A woman whose family has been in America for many generations uses a baby blanket as her altar cloth and on it has arranged a Coca-Cola bottle, a candle that has a picture of Our Lady of Guadalupe on it, and a stack of books.

Our ethnic heritage is important to who we are and how we present ourselves to the world. Creating something like the heritage tables at the diversity workshop is a way of honoring those who have come before us while also consciously making our heritage a part of who we are today. Because our ethnic heritage and our faith heritage are often inextricably linked, we can recognize and carry on the traditions of our culture on our home altar by including objects on it that reflect our heritage as well as our faith. If we come from cultures that have strong altar traditions, our altar may look similar to our grandmother's altar. If the family altar is new to our ethnic tradition, the presence of a Bible in the language of our ancestors, an icon from our family's country of origin, or a prayer book containing prayers specific to our homeland can bring historic faith traditions into present home worship.

Our ancestors in faith, whether from generations ago or in recent times, passed their traditions and beliefs on to us, helping create the person of faith we are today. The writer of the letter to the Hebrews speaks specifically of many saints of the Bible and their faith actions, yet he concludes that "none of them received what had been promised. God had planned something better for us so that only together with us would they be made perfect" (Hebrews 11:1–12:1). My faith is encouraged when I imagine Abraham, Sarah, Daniel, and Rahab standing in heaven waiting for me, but I also have Julian and Thomas, Laura and Forest to thank for my faith. Julian of Norwich lived several centuries ago, but her visions of God's love in dark times still speak to me today. Thomas à Kempis, likewise through his words of inspiration, seems a partner with me in my faith journey. Laura and Forest are my grandparents, who by their worship and service to others lived out their Christian faith in a way that urges me to do the same. These are my personal family-faith bearers without whom my faith might not be alive today. Many of us owe our faith to someone who came before us in history or in our family. Those witnesses, and the particular traditions they left us, deserve a place on our altars.

While we can include on our altar some representation of the traditions and faith bearers in our personal history, we can also learn from the traditions of other cultures in creating altars for our faith expression.

Many cultures have special home altar traditions, but we will explore three especially rich traditions here. First we will look at the home altar traditions in Latino Catholic culture, including the particularly popular traditions for Mexican Day of the Dead celebrations and *Viernes de Dolores*. Then we will examine two other special celebrations that revolve around the use of a home altar: *La Purisima* in Nicaragua and St. Joseph's Day in Italy. All three of these altar traditions are widespread not only in their home countries but also among immigrants to the United States, who have in turn passed them on to others. I offer them for anyone using a home altar who might wish to adopt aspects of these vibrant celebrations for their own home worship or who might be inspired by them to create special celebrations using their home altar.

Home Altars in Latin and Hispanic Cultures

In most of the countries which were at one time Spanish colonies and therefore strongly Catholic, a strong tradition of home altars has been in practice. This includes Mexico, Central and Latin America, the Caribbean, and the Philippines. Especially in remote rural areas, where priests were scarce and churches inaccessible, the faithful became dependent on home altars for worship.

Family altars are usually built around a table next to a wall in the main living area. They may also be in a bedroom, on a shelf, or the top of a dresser. Often a central item is a *Santo Nino* or Christ child, statue of Mary or statue of a patron saint. They may be ceramic, metal, wood, or plastic. Puerto Rico has developed a particularly rich tradition of *santos de palo* or saints of wood that are created specially for home altars. *Santeros*, or special wood carvers, create various images of saints and holy figures. In Mexico, *retablos* or Biblical scenes etched on tin, are common on family altars. Around the central image are candles to be lit during prayers, flowers (particularly the yellow marigold), prayer cards, and personal items. Often pictures of loved ones who have died are included on the family altar.

Through the oral tradition that accompanies these altars, stories about patron saints or long-ago family members are passed on, and both faith and family history are preserved. Many a child has seen his or her grandmother offering novenas or saying private prayers around such an altar. Some families gather around altars to say the rosary, sing, or pray on a regular basis. Often when leaving the home family members touch the saint and say a prayer as they leave. Altars in this tradition also promote hospitality, as they designate the home as God's space, which means that visitors are seen as sent from God and thus welcomed as part of the family.

Altars in Latin cultures are not passive but active, coming alive during worship times, on special feast days in the church, or during celebrations of a patron saint. At these times, items on the altar are replaced or rearranged. The altars may seem particularly alive at Christmas, when families often put together *nacimientos,* or Nativity scenes. With their physical representations, Latin home altars actively engage children in the faith life, encouraging them to remember the various stories of Jesus as well as those of the saints who have lived through church history.[1]

Sometimes for special ceremonies a priest will say a home Mass. For special occasions of worship in the home, a saint's statue from the church may be borrowed. In the Philippines, the home is often the mortuary and place of the funeral Mass. The family continues to offer prayers around the casket for two weeks before family and friends process to the cemetery for burial.

Latino immigrants to the United States brought their home altar traditions with them. Judy King, a sculptor who grew up in west Texas, says altars were commonplace in her largely Hispanic Catholic community, with everyone having one in his or her home. Many families had a patron saint, and a statue of the saint was placed in a prominent place on the home altar or in a shrine made specifically for it. Saints commonly honored by Tejano families are Nuestra Señora de Guadalupe, El Niño Jesús, and La Virgen de San Juan de los Lagos. Altars in these communities weren't just present in homes; they were also erected most anywhere as a remembrance of an everyday miracle or special event. Carolyn Ware, a professor at Louisiana State University, writes about the ethnic altars among Louisiana immigrants. She notes that Vietnamese immigrants have a special reverence for the Virgin Mary and families say prayers together several times a day. Often Chinese scroll paintings are hung near their altars, bringing their Vietnamese identity into their new lives. Home altar decorations among French Catholic immigrants may include a woven magnolia leaf or blessed palm branch above a doorway.

Day of the Dead

In many Latino cultures, a yearly celebration using altars occurs on November 1, All Saints' Day. Celebrated as *Día de los Muertos*, or Day of the Dead, this commemoration of those who have died centers on the preparation of elaborate altars, or *ofrendas*. A designated area in the home is cleared so that the altar can be set up there. The altar is generally a table but may also include overturned wooden crates covered with cloths to provide levels for decoration. Tradition has it that the spirits of loved ones who have died will come back on the Day of the Dead to visit, so families prepare to place on the table the favorite foods and drinks of those who have died. Pictures of the loved ones, from every stage of their life, as well as mementos of them are included on the altar. Decorations frequently include flowers, candles, paper cutouts, and candy skulls. Altars are often set up in the home days or weeks in advance of November 1, when families then go to the cemetery with flowers and food.

Often some members stay for all night vigils and large blankets spread with food for family picnics dot the cemeteries in Latin America for this remembrance. In Guatemala kites are flown as a way of reaching out to the dead. Remembrance in these cultures often continues on November 2.

A festive celebration of *Dia de Los Muertos* that I attended at a community center in Houston featured carefully constructed and creative altars made by many different participants. One altar paid tribute to a mother, with items that included an opened tube of lipstick and a perfume bottle on a silver tray from her dresser, as well as a collection of her sewing threads, needles, and buttons. Pictures of her when she was a young girl, as well as when she was a grandmother, were placed on the altar, along with flowers and bread. An altar dedicated to a man displayed jeans and work boots, a record album cover, oranges, and a cross. A group of teenagers from the Spanish club of the local high school had put together an altar to honor a classmate who had died four years earlier. A box with numerous cubicles exhibited pictures and memorabilia from each stage of his life. In one compartment were baby pictures, a pacifier, and a baby bottle; in another, there were preschool pictures, a copy of *The Tale of Peter Rabbit*, crayons, and an action figure. The last cubicle held pictures from his high school years, a lacrosse mitt, sports trophies, and signed baseballs. A letter that his sister had written about him and his qualities was placed on the altar as well, with copies for those who passed by. I could imagine the stories that must have been shared, with both tears and laughter, in the making of that altar.

While this tradition is particularly kept by those of Hispanic origin, setting aside a time to honor members of the family who have died is a wonderful possibility for all. Certainly many American families should be able to relate to altars that hold pictures of relatives who have passed away, since most of them have such a memorial on their refrigerator, in the array of photographs of family and friends both past and present. Putting pictures and mementos on our altar of relatives who have gone before us signifies the intention to give thanks for them and pray for them before God. American culture tends to sanitize life and avoid talk of death. The ritual of making commemorative altars provides a way to include death as a natural part of our lives through thoughtful planning, telling of stories, and collecting of items to honor those who have gone before us. The Day of the Dead celebration need not be elaborate; it could be a simple remembrance on November 1 at the family altar of all those who have died. This can be an opportunity for communication, for grieving, for healing, and for rejoicing together in keeping the memories and contributions of our family alive.

Viernes los Dolores

In Mexico, the Friday before Good Friday is another day in which home altars are specially set up. Altars are made in honor of Our Lady of Sorrows, with her image surrounded by crosses, flowers, candles, and sometimes figures representing the story of salvation.

In San Miquel de Allende, Mexico, public fountains are decorated and after Masses at the main churches, families travel door to door visiting creative and elaborate home altars. The altars may be set up in windows or open for inspection to visitors within the home. This is the day in which homes are most open to the public, much as in America homes are open to visitors on Halloween.

La Purisima and *La Griteria*

Nicaraguans have a special tradition of creating home altars during their celebration of Mary, the purest one, on the feast of the Immaculate Conception, *La Purisima*. Preparations begin nine days in advance of the feast day, which is December 8, with families making altars draped in cloths of blue, the color associated with Mary. Traditional foods, such as *gofios*, a candy of corn and brown sugar, along with fruits and decorations fill the altar. Purisimas are private parties held for a week in advance at which guests say the rosary and sing to the Virgin Mary. On the evening of December 7, the final day of the *novenanio*, a more public celebration or *La Griteria* (the shouting) is held in the community. People go from house to house asking loudly, "Who is the cause of this happiness?" and hosts call out, "the Immaculate Conception!" Visitors, both friends and strangers, are welcomed into the home and offered food and drink as everyone heartily sings traditional songs of praise to the Virgin Mary.

When Nicaraguans in the United States celebrate *La Purisima*, they might add touches from their land of residence. For instance, Nicaraguans in Miami place altars outside on the lawn as well as inside the house. They display the Virgin surrounded by potted plants and flowers or nestled in an existing tree or shrub, with Christmas lights and balloons adding to the festive decorations. In a discussion of immigrant traditions in New Orleans, Carolyn Ware describes a celebration of *La Purisima* in one Nicaraguan home:

> The elaborate altar . . . in the Keisling home is made on a dining room table covered with a blue cloth and curtains and draperies of blue satin; blue is the color traditionally associated with the Virgin. A treasured statue of the Immaculate Conception, brought from Nicaragua four decades ago, is placed high on a pedestal or chair on the altar and surrounded by candles, fresh and silk flowers, holy pictures, incense, clouds of tissue paper, and tiny lights. . . .

The infant daughters of family and close friends are sometimes asked to be "angels" on the altar. Dressed in white gowns with golden trim, foil wings and halos of flowers, toddlers are placed in high chairs at the side of the altar and the chairs are covered with tissue paper to create the effect of a cloud. Angels falling asleep on the altar, sucking their thumbs, or becoming restless detracts not at all from the ritual, as the Purisima is a celebration of family life and community as well as piety, and children are an important part of the event.[2]

La Purisima is a wonderful example of building a family faith tradition centered around a particular faith celebration that uses the home altar, includes children and adults, and reaches out in faith-filled hospitality.

St. Joseph's Altars

Many Italian families remember March 19 with a special feast honoring St. Joseph, their patron saint. The tradition began in the Middle Ages in Sicily. During a drought, the people prayed to St. Joseph and promised that if their prayers were answered they would honor him with a giant feast with food to be given to the poor. Their prayers were answered and thus began a yearly tradition in honor of St. Joseph that continues in many Italian communities still. A central part of the tradition involves building an altar to St. Joseph, which often consists of three levels, representing the Holy Trinity, draped in white linen and covered with flowers. A main table is laden with all sorts of special breads and food to be given to the needy. The altar also includes a Nativity scene and perhaps carpentry tools such as a saw, a hammer, and nails. Altars may be in individual homes or in a church parish or even in a whole neighborhood, sometimes taking months to prepare.

The altar is traditionally blessed on March 18, and afterward people can bring to the altar their own prayer petitions as well as offerings for the poor. Many of the foods that are prepared are nonperishable so that when the altar is taken down on March 19, the foods can be given to those in need. Sometimes the breaking of the altar comes after a reenactment of the holy family seeking shelter called *Tupa, Tupa,* which in Italian means "knock, knock." Children dressed as the holy family knock on three doors, seeking shelter and food. After the children are refused at the first two, the host at the third welcomes them. Because the feast is during Lent, no meat is prepared. However, elaborate breads called *cuccadati* are made in symbolic Christian forms such as a cross, fish, heart, lamb, dove, or crown of thorns. A latticework for the altar is covered with branches of myrtle, bay leaves, oranges, lemons, and the decorative breads.

St. Joseph's Day altars, *La Purisima* and *Viernes de Dolores* all illustrate the way in which a day of special faith importance can be celebrated using the home altar with rituals to make the occasion festive and focused on the saint. These home altar celebrations also include an aspect of hospitality and larger community festivity. Any family might use these models to create its own celebration around a particular person or event in faith history of significance to the family. A group of families in a faith community might work together to create home celebrations that are inclusive of others or that culminate in a community service.

Adopting Ethnic Traditions for Home Altars

Epiphany is the traditional time for the blessing of homes, and some African American parishes in Houston have developed a way of honoring this tradition. Families gather on Epiphany and begin the house blessing by writing the initials of the three wise men along with the current year above their door; thus, the year 2004 would be represented by the symbol "20CMB04" (C stands for Casper, M for Melchior, and B for Balthazar). After inviting God to bless the home in this way, they go around the house sprinkling each room with holy water and singing "We Three Kings." They then gather around their home altar for worship, with different family members assigned to different parts of the singing, reading, and prayers.

While these various altar traditions serve the purpose of faith education, and preservation for the people of their cultures, we do not necessarily have to come from a particular ethnic heritage to adopt some of its wonderful traditions. *Dia de Los Muertos* has begun to be celebrated much more widely than in just the Latino community as a way of remembering and honoring those who have died. Building St. Joseph's altars on March 19 can be a way for anyone to remember Joseph's story as well as the poor in our times of prosperity. *La Purisima* could be celebrated by a faith community as a way of opening their homes to one another and honoring Mary. And all of us who aim to keep our home God-centered might want to consider adopting a traditional Epiphany house blessing.

Additionally these rich ethnic celebrations provide examples of the varieties of ways to build family faith traditions around the home altar. We might all consider which biblical story or person speaks most strongly to our family, perhaps because a birthday falls on a saint's day or because a certain event is similar to a family challenge or vocation, and create a family celebration around that story. Different members of a family might each choose a story or person and take the lead in creating a new celebration. My hope is that the vibrant customs developed by those who have gone before and by those in countries with strong altar traditions will inspire all of us to imagine possible new ways to use our own home altars.

CHAPTER EIGHT

Outdoor Altars:
Worship in Nature's Temple

No matter what else is happening in your world,
and even when summer afternoons are scorchers,
you can still, like Adam and Eve, sneak out
in the cool of the morning and walk with God.
Find any woods, lake, meadow, or garden spot
and wander down whatever hillside, pounded path, or
thicket that calls your name that day until something
makes you cry uncle and stop to wonder—
like a threesome of trees that may have started
growing fifty years ago, when you and your two sisters
also had your birth, a patch of bursting Queen Anne's lace
mixed with delicate daisies, a cedar downed across a trickling
stream that invites a return with your six-year-old nephew,
berries presented like a good kindergarten teacher might,
at just the right hour for your morning snack, or a tulip poplar
that grew sideways at its base to reach the light but does not
topple because its roots hold it like fine tackles on a football field.
At each stop, declare Habakkuk's words,
"The LORD is in his holy temple;
Let all the earth keep silence before him."

In that silence, you might hear a titmouse twittering, a bee circling
until it lands, or the wind clapping the trees' hands for them.
You may join in the applause.

—In the Cool of the Morning

Just as the patriarchs spontaneously built an altar when God appeared to them, so too can we build an altar and worship when we are in God's creation and come across a sure sign of God's presence. Our signs of God's appearing are not the first-ever rainbow or a crossing of the Jordan before entering the Promised Land. Our signs are the ongoing evidence of a master artist whose delights led the psalmist to announce, "The heavens declare the glory of God; the skies proclaim the work of his hands" (Psalm 19:1). Our signs are what St. Paul referred to as the proof of God that we all see on a daily basis: "For since the creation of the world God's invisible qualities—his eternal power and divine nature—have been clearly seen, being understood from what has been made" (Romans 1:20). We do encounter miraculous signs of God's presence—the vastness of the night sky, the bright palette of colors of a setting sun, a possum waddling down a trail with its babies in tow—but just as often, our wonder can be aroused by a spiderweb suspended between two trees, or the peculiar and creative forms of a tree's branches, or the multiplicity of life represented in one square foot of grass.

Jacob used the stone his head had been resting on to build his altar; Joshua instructed his men to take stones from the Jordan riverbed for the building of his altar. In the same way, I sometimes make a small personal altar with materials at hand when I encounter God. I may place a pile of pebbles at the base of a magnificent tree, or I may stick a fallen forked branch into the ground and put a large leaf on top of it as a banner to indicate an animal crossing. At the beach, I may design artwork in the sand when I spot porpoises playing. These encounters between creature and Creator are a personal gift of God, and I respond with thanksgiving.

One Palm Sunday years ago, I walked out of the hunting cabin on my family's land in Virginia, full of emotion from a heated argument, and headed out to the woods. All the pent-up energy inside me propelled me forward until I was several miles into the heart of the forest. Eventually, I slowed, feeling safely alone, and I began to notice the sights around me. A huge flat rock on the side of the trail seemed to call out to me as a place to stop, to sit, to ponder, to pray. I cried out to God in both anguish over the fight and gratitude for a Savior who understood my heart. Across from me, I noticed a pile of stones. It seemed a natural beginning of an altar. I placed a few other stones on top of the pile and then looked around for two sticks to make a simple cross. My altar fashioned, I sat back down and began to sing out loud in this place where no one but God could hear, with a freedom and release that turned my emotions into exquisite joy. A song rose up in me from many years earlier: "Give me oil in my lamp, keep burning, give me oil in my lamp, I pray. Give me oil in my lamp, keep me burning. Keep me burning 'til the break of day. Sing hosanna, sing hosanna, sing hosanna to the king of kings." I realized I was celebrating Palm Sunday as I never had before, waving the palms of my emotions as I sang hosannas to the King of all Creation. No one else may ever pray in that spot again, but I still smile just remembering that best Palm Sunday ever. And I imagine that someday someone with a contemplative eye might spot that pile of stones across from the big flat rock and wonder if it was made for worship.

If altars are simply the meeting place for God and God's people, what likelier place for meeting God than in God's natural creation? When we are in need of spiritual refreshment and worship, we can go to a place that has God's signature all over the natural artwork. This can be a little city park, a vast national wilderness, or our own backyard. As we practice the lectio of life, we need not wait to get home to build an altar and give thanks. As we anticipate the places where our souls will regularly meet and worship God, we might want a more permanent altar in a setting designed by God.

Finding Spaces for Outdoor Altars

I often find outdoor places that draw me to them again and again. When my young family lived on the Upper West Side in New York, the park at the Cathedral of St. John the Divine became a regular destination for my young son and me. Our delight with the wildlife there caused us to refer to it as "Peacock Park." I would frequently sit on the same bench by a grassy spot where my son would chase birds or stoop to pick up bugs. It became an outdoor home to us in the city. If I were still living there today, I would use a ledge on the wall by the bench as my own outdoor altar. Before leaving the park for the day, I would place on that altar some offering of thanks to God for my soul refreshment of the day, such as a feather or leaf. The next time I returned, the altar might still contain a small pebble that would make me smile in remembrance, though the wind would have probably cleared the altar fresh for another filling.

For those who find God in nature, discovering a place in your community that inspires worship is helpful. Going to the same places over and over help our hearts return to God, just as they do with out home altars. When we find a comfortable log to sit on along a wooded path, we can mark it in some personal but unobtrusive way. We might find a branch on the ground with a cross-like T or any inspiring shape and post it into the ground upright. Or we might start a small pile of rocks, to which we could add a rock at every visit. In many rocky hiking places, cairns or rock piles are created to guide hikers where a trail is not obvious. A small pile of rocks at a familiar place for personal worship can become a spiritual cairn.

We don't have to create physical altars outside to have fulfilling worship experiences in nature. Sometimes just returning to a familiar place where we have received signs of God's presence can open up our hearts and inspire worship. In this way, the outdoor altar, being a secret spot known only to us, becomes an even more intimate place for meeting God. In Houston, like hundreds of other city dwellers seeking a large green space, I like to walk the three-mile path at Memorial Park. Most of the time my worship is in the walking rather than the stopping. However, there are a few places that help turn my thoughts to God because of encounters I have had there with the divine. Around one bend in the path and into the straightway beside the busiest road, I always look up at the sky. There, one day during my sister's worst time of battling cancer, I discovered the likeness of an angel in the clouds. A peace filled me, giving me assurance that God would care for us whether she lived or died.

At another place, the path goes through the woods, and here I look for berries on the bushes that speak to me of quiet celebration of the fruitfulness of life. Many of us have a regular walking path or special place to sit for quiet refreshment outside, at least for certain seasons. Wherever we go to walk or sit outside prayerfully, we can look for the signs of God to us that become ongoing symbols of God's particular presence on what we might see as our larger altar of life in the place of our regular worship.

An outdoor altar space can even be a place in our community that might not seem particularly conducive to worship but is nevertheless a place where we feel most attuned to God's ways. Sometimes I time my walking so that I arrive at a Beck's Prime restaurant in the park at sunset. After much scouring of this flat city to find a cleared space from which to view the sunset, I have discovered that the restaurant's patio, facing west out over a golf green, has the best unobstructed view for sunset watching. Though I have no permanent altar markings there, a chair turned to the straightway between tall pines at the hour of sunset becomes my personal outdoor altar.

While everyone can find some public space that can become a home base for outdoor personal worship, converting whatever outdoor space we have in our own backyard offers more permanent altar possibilities. Even if we don't have a backyard to call our own, we can create a space for worship in whatever outdoor space we do have. In an apartment, for example, a little window box can offer a touch of creation wonder. A small arrangement of flowers or herbs with a cross or wind chime nestled amongst the growth makes a pleasant small altar, especially if a comfortable chair is set up for looking out the window at that spot.

When I was looking for a space for my office, I found a house with rooms that had been converted into therapy offices. There was a first-floor space available that offered a horrible view onto the driveway and the wall of the resale shop next door. I asked the owners of the building if they might build a simple fence outside the window to block the view of the driveway. They agreed to that, and we planted a few vines to climb the fence and some heather to cover the ground, with a hibiscus and crepe myrtle for blooms. I hung an outdoor metal cross on the fence where only I can see it from my office chair position. Now, everyone thinks I have the best office view. Between clients or when I'm on my lunch break, I can roll over to the window and soak in the growing outdoor sights for meditation and relaxation.

If you happen to have even a little outdoor space and are willing to think creatively and work the dirt, you can create a simple outdoor worship space. A friend of mine who recently retired from her job is using her newfound time to create in her backyard a quiet, inviting space for prayer and meditation. She found a fountain made of clay pots that reminds her of Jesus' encounter with the Samaritan woman at the well and His offer to give us living water, and she made this the central element of her prayer space. Around the fountain, she has planted blood grass, wonderfully symbolic of Jesus' gift of both water and blood for our new life. With some additional plantings and a few spaces for sitting, she has created her own outdoor altar.

My family lives in a town house that has a small, enclosed outdoor courtyard. When we moved in, it had basically a tree, sandy bare soil, and a walkway. With the help of a carpenter, we added a patio with a table and swinging chair under the tree, and we made a little garden area in the four-by-eight-foot plot of ground. With a trickling water fountain surrounded by flowers in the middle of the plot and vines covering the back wall, it makes a great little meditation spot. I've added a plaque to the brick wall, garden bells, and bird feeders. Because the courtyard is enclosed, it actually is a more private outdoor altar space than a big yard might be.

A much larger plot of land where I have freedom to build outdoor altars is my family's farm in Virginia, which my grandfather bought years ago and left in part to my parents. When I visit, I often will just set off and wander in whatever direction the Spirit leads me, exploring new ravines and hillsides, looking for treasures of the Creator hidden across the land. I feel like a child in an Easter egg hunt, eagerly seeking to discover the wonders of a sunlit glade in the woods, protruding rock ledge, babbling brook, or mighty tree. This is my special outdoor practice of lectio of life.

I take inspiration from St. Francis, who retreated to the wooded mountain of La Verna in Italy for long hours or days in prayer. He and his fellow monks would find a spot in a cave or under a rock ledge or in a grove of trees where they would live and pray on the land. Simple spaces of God's own creating or simply designed sanctuaries in wooded spaces were the places of their early prayer.

When I discover what feels like a sacred place on my wanderings around the land in Virginia, I stop and pray. Several years ago, I made some simple prayer benches from salt treated pine, which I have carried to these prayerful places. A few people know where a prayer bench can be found. Other places are known only to me and God. In each space, I have cleared a bit of the brush and planted a few bulbs. Sometimes a natural wonder itself becomes the altar for my worship, such as a rock rising out of the earth in the middle of the woods, with a hole carved in it by water probably a thousand years ago.

In other spaces, I have designated a place for worship by creating a simple altar with materials at hand. My father showed me a wonderful walnut grove in the middle of the woods, and I have used logs I found there to form an outer circle with a bench for kneeling and a central altar. In a little sunlit glade amidst cedars, I have fashioned a mini-altar of stacked rocks and a cross of sticks. I imagine designing stations of the cross in a set of clearings in a distant wood. My sister and I have talked of one day using river rocks to outline a labyrinth. My hope is that over the years and generations, other family members as well as friends and visitors will also enjoy and contribute to these simple sacred spaces for worshipping our amazing Creator God.

Although I have a larger playground for outdoor lectio of life and altar building than many people due to my grandfather's hardwork and generosity, we all can find a place on earth that is particularly dear to us and use it for lectio of life and altar building in some way. For my sister, this is in Bar Harbor, Maine, where her family goes for her husband's summer biology research. For another friend, it is the high desert land in New Mexico where he hikes. The land may be a national or state park, a camping ground, a retreat house, or a friend's little cabin in a place of beauty. Each visit produces new places of particular spiritual discovery which can be marked in small personal ways or simply with mental pilgrim altars. Each time we return, the old secret places bring returning joy and the new discoveries ignite heartfelt gratitude anew.

Outdoor Altar Spaces Designed for Public Use

Some individuals and many retreat centers have built more elaborate and permanent outdoor spaces where people can worship. Driving in some places such as west Texas, New Mexico, Italy, or Mexico, personal shrines or little chapels sometimes can be spotted near the side of the road. Often they are dedicated to a particular saint or have a particular theme. They may be simply a wooden lean-to or three-sided stone structure with a central stone niche. Flowers often bloom from pots or little surrounding gardens. Although often designed by a particular family on their land, most of these faith-filled families are happy for travelers to add their prayers at a roadside worship space. Praying there, the traveler's imagination may conjure up pictures of farmers, craftsmen, and families with the blessings or miracles of their lives that produced such a shrine.

In retreat centers throughout the country, personal outdoor worship spaces have been designed for use by visitors. Endless variety comes out of natural materials used in natural settings to draw the wanderer into worship. For example, at Villa de Matel in Houston, a side path off a mile-long nature trail leads to an octagonal space with benches. In the center of the space is a large cross made of two cut logs nailed together and set in the ground. Mater Dolorosa, a retreat center nestled at the foot of the Sierra Madre overlooking the city of Los Angeles, has beautifully cultivated gardens that offer a stations of the cross walk. Each station has a large stone relief where people can meditate. In addition, there are small benches for rest and meditation, often near a statue of a saint set amidst the green growth of the gardens. Another circular walk at the retreat center has mosaic pictures at six stations that invite retreatants to meditate on the sorrows of Mary. An advantage of outdoor altars is the magnificent setting of God's creation, which invites wonder and awe far beyond that inspired by human creations. Whether simple or elaborate, outdoor altars can help turn the hearts of those who come in powerful ways to worship the Creator.

Creating Outdoor Altars

In a special spot of land, planned outdoor altars create ongoing welcoming spaces for worship. Creativity and variety are the key ingredients, so what follows are simply beginning ideas to help the imaginative worshipper create his or her outdoor altar space. Generally the following suggestions are for use on your own land, although owners of public space often gladly welcome creative donations for or help in creating outdoor meditation spaces.

Benches

Perhaps the first thing that welcomes a person to an outdoor worship space is a place to kneel or sit. A friend of mine in Virginia has an eye for beautiful, meditative spots. When she becomes aware of one in her neighborhood, she puts up a simple wooden bench where others can sit and enjoy the beauty as well. On a day soon after I discovered the incredible ancient oak on our family farm, I took her to admire it with me. The next time I visited Virginia, she gave me one of her benches to put up by the oak so that walkers for years to come can pause and wonder and pray. Her benches are made of two tree posts set in the ground with a flat piece of wood nailed across them. She hammers the seat onto one post with nails placed in the design of her initials and adds the initials of the receiver of the bench on the other side.

Benches can be as simple as a tree stump or stone in our yard or as elaborate as a wooden bench in which a word or verse of Scripture has been carved into the back or written on a plaque nailed to the bench. Before my son proposed to his fiancée, he ordered a bronze plaque for the back of a wooden bench that said, "Heather, will you marry me? I love you, Ben." The spot of this bench on a ridge at the Virginia farm, where he made his proposal, will be a place of joy for years to come. Whether engraved on a plaque or painted by hand on a piece of wood, words of a poem or passage from Scripture may inspire someone passing by to sit down and meditate.

Stones with Words

At a retreat center in southern California, a long, winding walk has been formed with bricks laid in a pattern around a series of flat stone blocks, each of which has a Scripture verse carved into it. When I visited the center, I would find a verse that particularly resonated with me and ponder it as I continued my steps. As I walked, another verse might jump out at me, and I would ponder it for the rest of my stroll. I could imagine as well just stopping and standing on a block to let the words sink into my soles and soul. I have in my little garden at home a stone with the message "The earth laughs in flowers." Many garden stores have stones with sayings to help mark an outdoor spot for reflection. Kits are also available for making your own poetry stones.

Plants

Specific plants are mentioned in the Bible and can symbolize different things.[1] In any outdoor space, plants can be chosen for their symbolic meaning. An Easter garden might have a cross surrounded by a bed of lilies, the symbol of resurrection and the flower mentioned in a description in the Song of Solomon of the place where lovers browse (2:16). Crocus bulbs could be the focus for a spring garden, representing the desert and wilderness blooming, as we read in Isaiah 35:1-2: "The desert and the parched land will be glad; the wilderness will rejoice and blossom. Like the crocus, it will burst into bloom; it will rejoice greatly and shout for joy." Meditation spots might be created around a tree or plant that is already present or that has been specially planted. A biblical passage inscribed on a plaque can be set near the tree or plant to encourage meditation. For example, a plaque with the words "Psalm 17:8, Keep me as the apple of your eye" could be placed by an apple tree. Psalm 1 might be inscribed on a plaque and placed near any strong, beautiful tree.

Sometimes plants, like items for a family altar, are chosen to represent people or events of sacred meaning. I have a friend who always plants violets in honor of her grandmother Viola and crepe myrtles for her grandmother Myrtle. Daffodils from my grandmother's garden make my sister's garden a place for holy and happy remembrance.

Central Altar

In an outdoor worship space, God often provides in Creation a central focus. A patch of flowers naturally blooming, a creek gurgling as birds sing overhead, or the sun or moon shining down from above, provides God's natural altar.

However, we are also made in the image of God the Creator and may wish to create a central altar in an outdoor worship space. Natural materials would be a large flat rock; a pile of rocks; a flat, topped tree stump; or a one to two-foot sawed piece of a large log turned up for a flat table top. The advantage of these central altars is that when we come to worship, they provide a place like our little tabletops at home upon which to put the small symbols of God. We might place there a white rock, a sprinkling of creek water, a fallen bird's nest, or a dogwood blossom.

Outdoor altars can be pilgrim altars, created and used on a single visit tramping through the woods one morning. Or they can be ongoing altars for personal or family use as we return to the same place over and over. There, as on our cloth-covered altars at home, we place symbols from our lectio of life and give heartfelt offerings of thanks. Each time we return again, we can remember the stories from the gathered tokens of praise to encourage our faithfulness through many seasons of life.

This past Thanksgiving I sat in the woods gazing up at a mighty oak tree. Though its bark and the acorns at my feet were similar to those of other oaks, this particular tree had two limbs stretching out on either side of it about twenty feet up. Both limbs were old, dead branches, now just extended stubs. They seemed on this cool fall day to be like hands reaching out to welcome me and my secret meditations on the hidden hillside. I dubbed the oak the "welcome tree," marked the spot, and will return again someday when I am in need of the warm, outstretched arms of God.

Home altars are like oak trees (or snowflakes or weasels or popcorn). They may have a familiar basic form that identifies them—a horizontal surface, probably covered with a cloth, containing various sacred (and seemingly not so sacred) items. But besides that, they are incredibly unique and personal. Each one bears the mark of its maker and its maker's own dance with the Creator of this wonderful, intricate world. Like a photo album of a couple's love relationship, the home altar might make a visitor wonder at strange objects that must have secret meaning or smile at an easily recognized delight. Like oak trees, altars grow and change with the seasons of the year and of a family's life.

My hope is that the ideas in this book have planted a seed for many individuals and families that will germinate and develop in wonderful ways. My prayer is that whatever your home altar looks like, it will be a tool in your life to help you pay attention to, thank, and remember the amazing, loving Creator of oak trees and every person in the world.

ACKNOWLEDGMENTS

My greatest inspiration for this book comes from Winnie Honeywell, director of the Office of Family Life Ministry, Diocese of Galveston-Houston, who not only first introduced me to the family altar through her own powerful presentation of it but has epitomized faithfulness in her work to support family faith development over many decades. Winnie had been struck by the power of the family altar when she heard about it from Wendy Wright, a professor at Creighton University. So to Wendy, who planted the seed, and to Winnie, who watered it into a flourishing flower for me to behold, I am most grateful.

Since being introduced to the concept of the family altar, I have sought ways to expand the possibilities for this powerful resource with others, teaching it in spiritual life and prayer workshops. I am grateful to the Community of Hope for their continued teaching of the family altar and giving me opportunities to share it more widely. When I have taught this curriculum over the past five years, I have been moved by the stories so poignantly shared by participants in the program. I thank them for their offerings. I also thank the Quechua women of Aramasi, Bolivia, who have produced for me and for others simple, colorful, handwoven, home altar cloths, which now grace our prayer spaces.

In the process of researching this book, I was helped by Alicia Perez, an associate of Winnie Honeywell's in the Office of Family Life Ministry; Bea Cunningham, associate director of the Office of Continuing Christian Education, Diocese of Galveston-Houston; and Sara Fontana, a family advocate in the same diocese. I am grateful to them for sharing their experiences and ideas for home altars for the readers of this book. Sara Fontana is one of the most passionate teachers of the family altar as a tool for enhancing the spiritual life of families and is available to bring it alive more personally for those wishing to have a workshop or retreat.

Within the Episcopal tradition, I discovered a sculptor, Judy King, who has given workshops on home altars, and I thank her for sharing her insights and ideas with me.

Finally, for the encouragement to write this book and for help along the pilgrim writing journey, thanks to my editor, Lil Copan. Thanks also to Laura Henry and Sharron Cox for personal editing help.

My greatest thanks go to the Creator God of life and every wonder within each home and along each step of our way, who gives us cause to praise Him with every breath and day.

ENDNOTES

Chapter 1

1. See also Romans 3:25, "God presented [Jesus] as a sacrifice of atonement, through faith in his blood," and Ephesians 5:2, "Live a life of love, just as Christ loved us and gave himself up for us as a fragrant offering and sacrifice to God."

2. Episcopal Church, *The Book of Common Prayer and Administration of the Sacraments and Other Rites and Ceremonies of the Church: Together with the Psalter or Psalms of David According to the Use of the Episcopal Church* (New York: Church Hymnal Corp., 1979), 335-36.

3. Mary Otto, "A Church away from Church," *The Washington Post*, Sunday, January 4, 2004, CO1.

4. See, for example, the web site of Palmyra, Pennsylvania, where the story of the historic Bindnagle Lutheran Church is recounted. Of the Germans who settled Pennsylvania, it is written, "These German settlers worshipped around family altars which soon became common altars." See http://www.palmyrapa.com/history/bindnagle.shtml.

5. Elizabeth Netto Calil Zarur and Charles Muir Lovell, eds., *Art and Faith in Mexico: The Nineteenth-Century Retablo Tradition* (Albuquerque: University of New Mexico Press, 2000).

6. Presbyterian Church in the U.S.A., "Pastoral Letter on Family Religion," in *The General Assembly of the Presbyterian Church* (Pub info: 1909), 122-23.

7. The Orthodox Presbyterian Church, *The Book of Church Order* (Willow Grove, PA: The Committee on Christian Education of the Orthodox Presbyterian Church, 1991).

Chapter 2

1. The epigraphs which appear at the beginning of this chapter and of chapters four and eight are excerpted from other writtings by the author.

2. Julia Cameron, *The Artist's Way: A Spiritual Path to Higher Creativity*, tenth anniversary ed. (New York: Tarcher Press, 2002).

3. David Rensberger, "Itinerant Every Day," *Weavings,* July/August 1998, pp. 39–46.

Chapter 3

1. For those interested in learning more about centering prayer, see Thomas Keating, *Open Mind, Open Heart: The Contemplative Dimension of the Gospel* (Rockport, MA: Element, 1992) or the resources of Contemplative Outreach Ltd. at http://www.centering-prayer.com/ or the World Community for Christian Meditation at http://www.wccm.org.

2. For example, the bookstore at Nativity of the Virgin Mary Greek Orthodox Church in Plymouth, Michigan (http://www.nativitygoc.org/BookStore/Info.htm) advertises, "Home altars are a necessity in every Orthodox home because we are Orthodox all week, not just one day each week. The bookstore stocks many home altar items for you. Home altar kits make excellent graduation presents for students, wedding gifts for the newlyweds' new home, adult baptism or house-warming gifts."

3. I have been knitting prayer shawls for several years as part of a growing ministry for those who are ill, dying, or in need. The ministry is described in Susan S. Jorgensen and Susan S. Izard, *Knitting into the Mystery: A Guide to the Shawl-Knitting Ministry* (Harrisburg, PA: Morehouse Publishing, 2003).

4. I will send one of the Bolivian altar cloths that I have purchased to anyone who makes a fifteen-dollar donation or more to Amistad Mission (see the Web site at http://www.AmistadMission.org), checks payable to Amistad Mission. Requests can be sent to Anne Grizzle, 2524 Nottingham, Houston, TX 77005.

5. The Catechesis of the Good Shepherd applies the principles of educator Maria Montessori to the spiritual formation of young children. Children often bring what they learn and produce home with them in profound ways. For more information, see the Web site of the National Association of the Catechesis of the Good Shepherd at http://www.cgsusa.org/.

6. See Domestic–Church.com for references to various documents, teachings and practical ideas for developing faith in the home.

7. For example, see Rev. John Wagner, "Restoring the Family Altar" (sermon, Covenant Free Presbyterian Church, Lexington, SC, April, 6, 2003), available at http://www.sermonaudio.com. See also "Sacred Spaces, Sacred Places: Worshipping the Lord at the Family Altar," by Kelly Haack previously available at LCMS.org.

8. Wagner, "Restoring the Family Altar."

9. "Sacred Spaces, Sacred Places: Worshipping the Lord at the Family Altar."

10. Susan S. Larson, "Marriage Stability Aided by Spirituality," review of research in David B. Larson and James P. Swyers, "Do Religion and Spirituality Contribute to Marital and Individual Health?" in *Marriage, Health, and the Professions: If Marriage Is Good for You, What Does This Mean for Law, Medicine, Ministry, Therapy, and Business?*, ed. John Wall et al. (Grand Rapids, MI: William B. Eerdmans 2002), 283B92. Research report available at the International Center for the Integration of Health and Spirituality, http://www.icihs.org/programs/researchreports/web/february.cfm.

11. Kenneth Kremer, "Home Worship," *Parish Leadership*, Fall 1998.

12. Sacredheartbookshop.com offers ideas on creating a home altar for Catholic families, noting, "The faith of the family should be displayed in the home. There should be a prominent place of worship. To decorate the houses with religious pictures is a custom as old as Christianity itself, for the true Christian has always considered his home as nothing less than a Temple of God, and the religious pictures as means to extend and preserve the spirit of Christianity in the home." See http://www.sacredheartbookshop.com/Web.htm.

13. Good resources include *Shared Silence* by Guinilla Norris, *Call to the Center* by M. Basil Pennington, *Kneeling in Bethlehem* by Ann Weems and *The Vigil* by Wendy Wright.

Chapter 4

1. For additional resources on *lectio divina*, see M. Basil Pennington, *Lectio Divina: Renewing the Ancient Practice of Praying the Scriptures* (New York: The Crossroad Publishing Company, 1998), Thelma Hall, *Too Deep for Words: Rediscovering Lectio Divina* (New

York: Paulist Press, 1988) and Norvene Vest, *Bible Reading for Spiritual Growth: A HarperCollins Resource for Small Groups and Individuals* (San Francisco: HarperSanFrancisco, 1993).

2. Thich Nhat Hanh, *The Miracle of Mindfulness: A Manual on Meditation*, rev. ed., trans. Mobi Ho (Boston: Beacon Press, 1987); *The Long Road Turns to Joy: A Guide to Walking Meditation* (Berkeley, CA: Parallax Press, 1996).

3. Tilden Edwards, *Sabbath Time* (Nashville, TN: Upper Room Books, 1992).

4. Julian of Norwich, *Revelations of Divine Love*, Westminster Cathedral/Abbs, manuscript, chapter 5.

5. Brother Lawrence, *The Practice of the Presence of God* (Springdale, PA: Whitaker House, 1982).

6. Jean-Pierre de Caussade, *The Sacrament of the Present Moment*, trans. Kitty Muggeridge (San Francisco: Harper & Row, 1982). This concept is given a more modern examination in Spencer Johnson, *The Precious Present* (Garden City, NY: Doubleday, 1984).

7. Rainer Maria Rilke, *Letters to a Young Poet*, trans. Stephen Mitchell (New York: Modern Library, 2001).

Chapter 5

1. Dennis Linn, Matthew Linn, and Sheila Fabricant Linn, *Sleeping with Bread: Holding What Gives You Life* (Mahwah, NJ: Paulist Press, 1995).

Chapter 6

1. For further information on ethical wills, see Jack Riemer and Nathaniel Stampfer, eds., *So That Your Values Live On: Ethical Wills and How to Prepare Them* (Woodstock, VT: Jewish Lights Publishing, 1991), or visit http://www.ethicalwill.com.

Chapter 7

1. Teresa Malcolm, "Creating Sacred Space," *National Catholic Reporter*, November 14, 2003.

2. Carolyn Ware, "Ritual Spaces in Traditional Louisiana Communities: Italian, Nicaraguan, and Vietnamese Altars," Louisiana's Living Traditions, Folklife in Louisiana, Louisiana Division of the Arts, http://www.louisianafolklife.org/LT/Articles_Essays/creole_art_ritual_spaces.html.

Chapter 8

1. A lengthy description of many of the plants in the Bible and their scriptural references can be found in Merrill F. Unger, *The New Unger's Bible Dictionary*, rev. and updated ed., ed. R. K. Harrison (Chicago: Moody Press, 1988). "Vegetable Kingdom" pp. 1325–41. See also "Good Shepherds of the Land," by Jane Austin McKeon, *Better Homes and Gardens*, Summer 2003, 98–105.

Books

Anderson, Herbert, and Edward Foley. *Mighty Stories, Dangerous Rituals: Weaving Together the Human and the Divine.* San Francisco: Jossey-Bass, 1998.

Boyer, Ernest, Jr. *Finding God at Home: Family Life as a Spiritual Discipline.* San Francisco: Harper and Row, 1984.

Caldwell, Elizabeth. *Making a Home for Faith: Nurturing the Spiritual Life of Your Children.* Cleveland, OH: Pilgrim Press, 2000.

Fuchs-Kremer, Nancy. *Parenting as a Spiritual Journey: Deepening Ordinary and Extraordinary Events into Sacred Occasions.* Woodstock, VT: Jewish Lights Publishing, 1996.

Hays, Edward. *Prayers for the Domestic Church: A Handbook for Worship in the Home.* Rev. ed. Easton, KS: Forest of Peace Books, 1989.

Howard, Thomas. *Splendor in the Ordinary: Your Home as a Holy Place.* Manchester, NH: Sophia Institute Press, 2000.

Hunt, Jeanne. *Holy Bells and Wonderful Smells: Year-Round Activities for Classrooms and Families.* Cincinnati, OH: St. Anthony Messenger Press, 1996.

National Conference of Catholic Bishops. *Catholic Household Blessings and Prayer.* Washington, DC: United States Catholic Conference, 1988.

Nelson, Gertrud Mueller. *To Dance with God: Family Ritual and Community Celebration.* New York: Paulist Press, 1986.

Vogt, Susan, ed. *Just Family Nights.* Elgin, IL: FaithQuest, 1994.

Web Sites

Domestic-church.com, a family apostolate, www.domestic-church.com.

Familyandchurch.com, produced by the Family Life Ministers of the Catholic Dioceses of Wisconsin, www.familyandchurch.org.

Homefaith.com, a service of Claretian Publications, www.homefaith.com.